DEVELOP YOUR LATENT PARANORMAL POWERS

An 11 Lesson Course On Crystal Gazing Clairvoyance, De-materialization, Seeing Through Solid Objects...And Learning To Excel At Other Fascinating Forms Of Supernatural Phenomena

Dragonstar And Sir William Walker Atkinson

Develop Your Latent Paranormal Powers

An Eleven Lesson Course On Crystal Gazing, Clairvoyance, De-materialization, Seeing Through Solid Objects...And Learning to Excel At Other Fascinating Forms of Supernatural Phenomena Expanded Edition

By Dragonstar And Sir William Walker Atkinson

Global Communications/Inner Light Publications

LET THERE BE LIGHT

INNER LIGHT PUBLICATIONS

Develop Your Latent Paranormal Powers
An Eleven Lesson Course
Expanded Edition

By Dragonstar and Sir William Walker Atkinson

Timothy Green Beckley: Editorial Director

Carol Ann Rodriguez: Publishers Assistant

Tim R. Swartz: Editor

Sean Casteel: Associate Editor

William Kern: Associate Editor

Cover Graphics: Tim R. Swartz

For Free Subscription To The Conspiracy Journal Write:

Tim Beckley/Global Communications

Box 753, New Brunswick, NJ 08903

Email: mrufo8@hotmail.com

www.ConspiracyJournal.Com
www.TeslasSecretLab.Com

CONTENTS

Dragonstar

Develop Your Latent Paranormal Powers

Your Journey Has Begun

Much has been written about the world of psychic phenomena and the powers of the human mind and its wide reaching potential. Even our astronauts have sent telepathic waves from the surface of the moon to see if someone on earth could read their minds.

ESP is sort of "old hat." We've all seen movies like **Ghostbusters** and **Mothman Prophecies** and fully realize and that there is an entire invisible universe that surrounds and permeates us. These energies extend beyond what we know as the material world and we can tap into these mystic forces to create and maintain our desires and goals.

Years ago, my co-author Sir William Walker Atkinson discovered the many possibilities of paranormal powers. He was well ahead of his time as this ll lesson study course plainly shows. But I, Dragonstar the living master of a clan of magicians whose roots extend back to the ancient land of Atlantis will now reveal secrets of our paranormal world to further promote the possibilities of the supernormal, psychic abilities, and the supernatural.

These amazing powers are available to all who are willing to throw off the shackles of our everyday lives and lift the veil that hides the unlimited potentials that the universe has waiting for us. Before you start, take ten minutes to meditate on the cover of this book. Ask yourself what it is you want out of life and what kinds of paranormal powers that you want to develop and use. Now, as you read these words, you are already being infused with the white light of unlimited universal energy.

Our lives were meant to be lived and enjoyed to their fullest. But usually we become so caught up in the everyday trivialities of day-to-day living that we lose sight of what is really important. Most of us go about our daily lives in a sort of stupor. We live like robots that have been programmed to preform the same functions day after day with no deviation from the program. We are asleep at the wheel with no desire to awaken and take control.

This is no way to live. Every day should be a new and different experience and we should greet it with the same excitement and expectations as a child greets Christmas morning or a trip to their favorite amusement park. We must shake ourselves awake and look about at the wonderful universe that we helped create and acknowledge how important a role we play.

You are now ready to begin your journey to enlightenment and spiritual growth. With this growth come great powers and abilities that seem almost too fantastic to

Develop Your Latent Paranormal Powers

believe. Abilities such as contacting the ascended masters, mind reading, telekinesis, astral journeys to other worlds, time travel and much more.

Read carefully the contents of the amazing book – for once you begin your quest, you cannot go back, you will not want to go back. Your old life will seem like a hazy dream, without focus or purpose. While your new life will be filled with incredible adventures and a new, more vivid way of looking at the world around you.

Contacting The Ascended Masters

One of the first things that you should do on your journey to enlightenment is to learn how to contact the Ascended Masters. These are highly advanced spiritual beings who are waiting to act as guides to those who are ready to grow and develop as enlightened beings of spiritual energy.

The Ascended Masters are available to everyone who asks for their help. You do not need to be an experienced channel or be a person who is well versed in spiritual matters for them to help you or teach you. They will always do their best to help you meet your goals for spiritual advancement and to help you with any problems that you have in your life in any way that they can.

Anyone can learn to channel. Channeling is a matter of opening to the love, energy, and conscious connection of a higher dimensional being. It is a tool that can be used in many ways. It is not only for relaying information.

When you meditate and feel the energy and love of your higher self or a guide, you are channeling. You are channeling their energy, even if you do not receive a conscious word or thought from them. Most people channel and receive guidance and information from their higher self or a guide and are not aware that they are channeling.

Many people receive information or guidance in the dream state or through sudden inspirational thoughts. Some people channel while they are working on art, music or other creative expressions. Most people experience this form of channeling in their everyday lives. People have always been able to channel. It is not a new or recent phenomenon. The Bible and other Holy books are full of channeled material and channeling experiences.

All people are spiritual beings who are a part of a very advanced higher self. Each person is very connected to their higher self, even if it is not a very conscious connection. Anyone can learn to channel and open that connection, not only to their higher self, but to all higher dimensional beings and to all that is.

There is nothing to fear when you channel. If it is your intention to open to your higher self and work only with them, then only your higher self will be there with you while you are reaching out to them. The higher self connection is a very powerful

Develop Your Latent Paranormal Powers

one. It is very helpful to establish a good higher self connection before channeling other beings.

It is a good idea to always ask your higher self to help you when you channel others. They can help you to establish a channeling connection with any higher dimensional guide or teacher that you wish to work with. So there is no need to fear that you will get into contact with a being that you do not wish to talk to.

Your higher self can make sure you are connected with the being you want to work with. You do have free will and can talk to anyone that you want, but we strongly suggest that you always work through your higher self, and only with your own guides or very advanced universal teachers.

If you are channeling a guide with the help of your higher self it is easier to make the connection with that guide. Working through your higher self also helps you to interpret the information given by a guide in a clearer way. Your higher self knows you better than anyone. If you are getting the information from a guide or universal teacher through your higher self, they can more easily help put the information into words and ideas that you can more readily understand and accept.

Your intentions and requests have everything to do with what happens when you channel. It is best to have in mind whom you want to work with and what kind of work that you wish to do before you start to channel. Each time before you start to channel or meditate, invite in whom you wish to work with and state what you want to accomplish in that session.

Learning to be a channel for universal or spiritual information to share with others may not be what everyone would like to do. But each person can learn to channel the love and energy of their higher self and other higher dimensional beings. Each person can establish a very conscious connection with their higher self, guides and Ascended Masters, for their own information and spiritual growth and help in their everyday lives.

There are many ways that you can learn to channel for information. One of the easiest is to simply sit quietly and ask that your higher self or a guide connect with you consciously and energetically. Once the connection is made, try to be as open as you can be to the thoughts and words that they will send you. You can just be aware of the thoughts and words, or you can repeat the information that you are getting out loud. If you are comfortable with it you can ask to connect with them in a more complete way and have them speak through you.

When you have established a good conscious connection with your higher self or guide and are comfortable channeling them, you can ask to work with a universal teacher, such as an Ascended Master or Archangel. The process is the same whether you are channeling your own higher self or any other higher dimensional being. It is no harder to channel an Ascended Master or an Archangel than it is to channel your

Develop Your Latent Paranormal Powers

higher self. They will always come to you in a way that you are ready for and capable of.

As you learn, grow, and develop your channeling abilities they can come to you in more and more expanded ways, but right from the start you can work with their energy and benefit from their love and guidance. The more that you accept yourself as the spiritual being that you are and an extension of your higher self, the easier it will be to open to the love and wisdom that is available to you. That frame of mind opens your consciousness and prepares you to work with your higher self, guides, and all universal teachers in a much more expanded way.

The Art Of Psychic Mind Reading

This hidden power is available to those who recognize and accept that there is a higher realm of knowing and communication beyond their own physical bodies. The universe is full of this unlimited energy that can be tapped by almost anyone who will make the effort to focus and tune themselves to its subtle vibrations. These vibrations are not just for the so called 'gifted' persons, but for everyone who makes the effort to learn its secrets.

Most all psychic people are that because they recognized the signs of this energy and focused their attention on its workings which is the very thing that is required in order to develop it. If they hadn't focused their attention on it, then they wouldn't be what they are.

To begin tuning into this force you need to learn about focusing. Focusing on even the smallest instance of psychic phenomena that happens to your self and to people around you. Play the event around in your mind continually, to get familiar with the sense of the action and presence of the energy involved. This will give you a perception of how involved and integrated is the underlying hidden power that caused the event to take place.

One of the most important things to understand is that every living thing, plants, animals, people, has consciousness and is connected to everything else in the universe. People, animals and plants are all connected to the hidden energy of universal consciousness that permeates the entire universe and 'wires' all of us together.

Understanding and accepting this simple concept is the most important requirement to developing one's own latent ability. The next important requirement, is that the person must have both a desire and willingness to develop and tune themselves so they can also connect with the universal spirit

ESP – Extrasensory perception is the term used to describe a means of getting

IV

Develop Your Latent Paranormal Powers

information from other than the five senses that everyone uses as their primary means. The five senses are seeing, feeling, smelling, tasting, and hearing. These are considered to be our 'normal' senses and any sense or gathering of information is said to be extra, or out of the ordinary.

When a person develops their ESP, they have increased their mind power by a quantum leap above other people. It enables them to send and receive information almost at will to influence things that are important to them.

Mind reading, clairvoyance, precognition are all perceived through mental telepathy. Mental telepathy makes possible the "knowing" about past future or current events that is not supposed to be part of our knowledge. When someone demonstrates an ability to send and receive information that is not part of their five ordinary senses, it is placed in the realm of "extra" almost as though it was bizarre or abnormal and not part of the human psyche or sense abilities. However, telepathic ability is available to all those willing to practice and learn how to increase this talent that is given to everyone at birth.

This is how clairvoyants, psychics and mediums know secret and private information about another person's life and are able to advise them. Some of them discovered that they had the ability at a young age and some not until later in their life. But they all have one thing in common. They made a decision not to ignore it, but rather to improve and cultivate it through patience, practice and effort. Many people can now benefit from their diligence and persistence in their own self development.

To become a psychic mind reader you must learn to switch your mindset from yourself and onto another person as the center point. Your focus is centered on the inner workings of that person as it relates to the world they live in. For this you need to go within to engage that part of yourself that communicates with the universal mind where all knowledge resides.

Just like learning any other skill you need to practice. Nothing comes to anyone without practice and reading another person is no different. Remember, you already have the ability, you only need to tune it and refine it. Mind set is important. The more serious you are about it, the faster you will develop your ability to give readings. If you are dedicated to learn, you will. Just remember, Rome was not built in a day, so be patient. Becoming a psychic mind reader requires patience and practice.

Meditation puts you on the fast track to developing your own potential. It helps you get in that deep inner part of yourself where you get help from outside – from the universal mind. If you don't meditate, you can still learn, but it takes a bit longer. Profound and meaningful information is more readily available for a person that meditates.

Develop Your Latent Paranormal Powers

As each person goes through life, the events of that life are recorded. Every thought, words spoken, actions taken and not, are recorded with the universal mind. Some psychic readers refer to this as the Akashic Records, but its easier to visualize it as a video recording. This is information that you as a psychic reader can access.

The information comes through 5 sources: **1. *Feelings*** - feelings that something is so, feelings of what a person is feeling inside, feelings about what a person fears, what is going on in their life, feelings about what is going on in regard to their personal relationships, etc.

2. *Pictures* - Visual pictures will come to the psychic reader, some are directly interpreted and others are indirectly related. That is some pictures are symbols for another meaning. For example: in giving a reading, a woman client is visualized fishing off a bridge. Does it mean that the client is really going to go fishing or is she looking for a man? The answer lies in developing a 'feel' of how to interpret these symbols. And in this case, it turned out that the client was looking for a man.

3. *Hearing* - The psychic mind reader hears words in the form of mind talk. As though the psychic reader was talking to herself. Sometimes it seems like words are being imagined by you, the mind reader.

4. *Knowing* - One of the most profound ways that a psychic reader gets information is through 'knowing.' Suddenly, information appears. And as if by magic, the reader knows something that she didn't know a moment earlier.

5. *Smelling and tasting* - The psychic reader gets a sense (feels) of smelling or tasting.

Sometimes you will only get a single word or picture about a person which doesn't provide a clear meaning. You must then go back and ask that symbol to give you more information. More information usually comes through one of the other sources. For example, the picture of the woman fishing on the bridge didn't give an explanation beyond the image itself. When the reader went back for more information, a feeling came to her that the woman was really actively looking for a man to be in her life. The psychic mind reader goes back to the source as many times as necessary to get a coherent message for her client.

Spiritual growth is the by-product of psychic development. As you expand you own awareness of the universe through the experiences you get from these practices, you become more balanced and discerning. You will see the world and people from a different perspective. You'll see things as a whole rather than from their individual parts. And you will have a greater empathy because you'll understand what is going on in many people, even if they don't see it themselves.

Every day of our lives we engage in the paranormal practice of communicating with a higher realm of consciousness and we are not even aware of it. Following is a list of things that everyone has experienced at least once. Look them over and

Develop Your Latent Paranormal Powers

remember similar such psychic events that happened to you. Once you have become aware of them, practice them and more will occur. Through a higher awareness you can make the paranormal become the normal for you.

Here are a few types of events you should be looking for: **1. Coincidences** - Pay attention to coincidences that amaze you, including those that don't. All coincidences have a meaning, especially if they seem to further your psychic or spiritual path. Record all of them. **2. Hunches** - See what happens with your hunches. Take the effort to see if they play out as they came to you. **3. Urges** - Follow up on urges. If you followed the urge, what happened? Did your inner urge match reality? **4. The little inner voice** - Listen to it. Deep within it gives you an awareness and knowledge about yourself or someone else. About the present, past or future. We don't always hear it, because our conscious minds are preoccupied with ourselves. The subtlety of this voice sometimes makes us think that our mind is talking to itself. Record these occasions, because this practice will greatly enhance your ability to hear more of this voice. **5. Predictions** - If you are going to see someone that you've never met, try to picture in your mind what this person looks like. Practice advance awareness, by always trying to predict things in advance of seeing or experiencing them. This is a good method for getting immediate feedback.

Invisibility - The Art Of Not Being Seen

Even though we are social creatures – all of us at one time or another desires the liberation of solitude and anonymity. The freedom, the power of not being seen, to be invisible, has charmed and challenged many throughout the centuries. Magicians, prophets, and philosophers alike have delved into the eternal mysteries seeking answers to the enigma of invisibility.

The concept of invisibility may have been confined to the world of myths and children's fairy tales if not for a few hints and anecdotal tales of deliberate and spontaneous cases of invisibility. Despite skeptical pronouncements on the impossibility and sheer silliness on the reality of invisibility – some claim that the power is very real, and accessible to those willing to learn the secrets.

Researcher and writer Donna Higbee has chronicled a number of interesting reports of people who seem to have a natural ability toward invisibility. Their paranormal power appears to operate without conscious effort. Much to the chagrin of the person involved. Most, however, had reported an interest in paranormal powers and meditation.

Higbee relates the interesting story of a woman named Vera (pseudonym) who had driven her car to the post office to get stamps. She walked in and joined the line,

Develop Your Latent Paranormal Powers

taking the end position. Soon thereafter a man walked in and asked the man directly in front of Vera if this was the end of the line.

The man ahead of Vera answered that he was indeed the end of the line, wherein Vera spoke up and said she was the end of the line. No one looked at Vera or acknowledged that she had spoken. In fact she was almost stepped on as the second man took up the end position in line. Vera thought to herself how rude and impolite these people were and moved slightly to the side of the line, so as not to be jostled; she continued moving up with other people.

When her time came to go to the counter to be helped, she walked up and stated her business and quite to her amazement, the man behind her walked right up and did the same. The postal clerk never acknowledged Vera but began assisting the man. Vera announced loudly that she was there first, but no one paid the slightest attention to her. It was as if she was a ghost, unable to be seen or heard.

Getting very upset by this time with what she considered extreme rudeness, she just walked out of the post office and went home. A number of days later, she was attempting to get some assistance in a store and no one would help her or even acknowledge that she was present. It seemed as if she was invisible to people around her and also couldn't be heard when she spoke. She had no idea what was happening, and certainly wasn't pleased about the entire situation.

Another woman reported to Higbee that she had been seated on the sofa, letting her mind wander as she stared at the wall. The wall seemed to take on a less-than-solid form and she was fascinated with it. When she finally came out of her reverie, she was astonished to find her husband searching the house for her and she certainly had not been there. Here, again, although she was physically present, she seemed to be unseen by another person.

Professor Vladimir Porshnev in his 1974 book ***About Early Human History*** speculates that early humans had the ability to activate the phenomenon of invisibility. Excessive psychic, nervous or physical strain can trigger spontaneous, natural invisibility. This does not produce complete physical disappearance, but invisibility vis-a-vis the observer. Professor Porshnev concluded that humans have lost this and similar abilities as a result of the increasing complexity of the human psyche.

It would seem then that invisibility is possible under the proper conditions and state of mind. Magicians have sought the perfect spell or rituals to ensure consistent invisibility time after time. One such spell was developed along the lines of making you less noticeable to those around you.

You should first visualize a white or black light (whichever one is more suitable to you) and visualize yourself inside that light, now picture that light getting blurry and taking in the colors of the objects around you, now see yourself getting blurry or

Develop Your Latent Paranormal Powers

being sucked into the light and the light taking the form of the objects around you until the light has completely become transparent.

You now fade into the light, becoming a part of it, until you completely disappear into the camouflage of the circle of light around you. This spell works pretty well. Although you won't actually be invisible to the naked eye, people will merely ignore you unless you touch them. Practitioners of this spell report that they can go right up to someone and not be seen until they touch them. People don't acknowledge that you're there, even though your in plain sight so to a certain extent, you are invisible.

Madame David-Neel explained in her book, *Magic and Mystery in Tibet*, that if you walk among crowds shouting and bumping into people you will make yourself quite visible. But, if you walk noiselessly, touching no one, looking at no one, you may be able to pass without being seen. Animals do this all the time to catch prey. It has also been pointed out that if you sit motionless you can cut down on your visibility.

However, there is a drawback to this method. Your mind generates noise. David-Neel says, "The work of the mind generates an energy which spreads all around the one who produces it, and this energy is felt in various ways by those who come into touch with it."

The idea is to cut off that source of energy, or noise. If this can be done, you become as silent as anyone can be. You may still be seen. That is, a camera or mirror would pick up your image, but you would not be noticed.

Said one expert: "When the mind inhibits emanation of its radioactivity it ceases to be the source of mental stimuli to others, so that they become unconscious of the presence of an Adept of the Art, just as they are unconscious of invisible beings living in a rate of vibration unlike their own."

Aleister Crowley wrote: "The real secret of invisibility is not concerned with the laws of optics at all. The trick is to prevent people noticing you when they would normally do so."

Apparently, Crowley had the power to keep people from noticing him. In an experiment, he took a walk along a street dressed in a golden crown and a scarlet robe. Despite his wild costume, he did not attract attention to himself.

Eliphas Levi points out: "A man, for example, pursued by murderers, after having run down a side street, returns instantly and comes, with a calm face, toward those who are pursuing him, or mixes with them and appears occupied with the same pursuit. He will certainly render himself invisible. The person who would be seen is always remarked, and he who would remain unnoticed effaces himself and disappears."

Tibetan Tantra Yoga teaches much, and in detail, about the art of invisibility. It declares that it is a matter of shape-shifting of the bodily form. Through direction of

Develop Your Latent Paranormal Powers

a subtle mental faculty or psychic power, whereby all forms, animate and inanimate, including man's own form, are created, the human body can either be dissolved, and thereby made invisible, by magically inhibiting the faculty, or be mentally imperceptible to others, and thus equally invisible to them by changing the body's vibration.

The mind can inhibit emanation of its radioactivity, and thus cease to be mental stimuli to others, so they become unconscious of the presence of that person. We are always unconscious of many invisible beings living in different vibratory expressions than our own.

The process according to Evans-Wents, who wrote and translated several books on Tibetan Tantra Yoga, is "giving palpable being to visualization," as an architect makes his two-dimension plans three dimensional, but in reverse.

So for the novice, learning to be invisible entails quieting ones mind to the point that you are no longer noticed. You haven't become transparent to light, but you no longer register on the minds of those around you. To practice this paranormal power you need to sit quietly, and close your eyes. Allow your consciousness to slowly turn inward. Believe it or not, this does not require any effort. It's a natural and involuntary process.

The first step is to blot out your environment. Make yourself oblivious to it. Next, keep in your mind the thought that you want to hide. Do this even though you may be sitting in an open room with other people around. Finally, eliminate all thoughts from your mind. This is probably the hardest thing for most people to accomplish, emptying all thoughts from your mind. Most of us find that our minds are almost always working. When we attempt to clear our heads, thoughts and images flood in at a fantastic rate.

To try and clean your mind of intruding thoughts, try concentrating on one particular thing. If you are of a religious mind, try the image of Jesus. Others have reported success with visualizing a clear, white light. Others like to form a pentagram with their mind. Whatever your choices, remember, the goal is to remove all thought from your mind. Remember, thoughts produce energy, and energy makes you more visible. Stop thinking, remain motionless with eyes closed, and you become invisible, not in the literal sense of the word, but unnoticed.

J.H. Brennan has devised a method to stop thought-energy. He says that if he cannot stop himself from shouting, he can conceal himself from you by surrounding himself with a soundproof screen that shuts out the noise. He uses the word "shouting" to mean "thinking." There is a technique for doing that and it is taught by the AMORC Rosicrucians.

Develop Your Latent Paranormal Powers

The Veil Of Obscurity

With this technique you can actually produce real invisibility. The Rosicrucians advise you to sit quietly as though you are meditating. Close your eyes. Now imagine that you are completely surrounded by a soundproof screen. Think of it as a curtain hanging down all around you, completely concealing you. Think of the curtain until you can feel its presence, keeping in mind that the curtain will make you invisible to others.

How can you tell if your experiment is successful? Simple. Place a mirror at the opposite side of the room, beyond the Veil's influence. You will be able to see through the curtain, but outsiders will not be able to see in. If you are successful, you will not see your image in the mirror.

However, don't hope for success immediately. Give yourself plenty of time to achieve it. Be patient, and never become discouraged. Acquiring occult powers is not easy. You can be sure that those who are successful are those who have enormous patience.

Shadowing

One more technique that is worth mentioning is shadowing. To shadow yourself you must absorb all manner of visible light rays. This means that if you must not allow any part of your body to reflect light. What must happen in order for the shadow effect is that the green reflection must be stopped. To do this, visualize yourself as a magnet for the visible light spectrum. The idea here is to not allow any light to be reflected from your skin, hair, clothing, etc. You should appear as a black or dark grey shadow. For more information on this subject, see the book: ***Invisibility and Levitation***, by Commander X, (1998).

Control The Things Around You

This paranormal power is for all of you who want to find a way to be in control of your personal energy/power, and haven't a clue how to start on the path. Energy weaving will show you how to direct and control your energy, as you receive it from other people, send it to other people, and send it through objects. Energy weaving is simply the exchange of power/energy. There should only be two people at a time who should attempt this energy exchange. This is until you are more in tune with your own powers/energy, and the energies of the others. You and a friend should

Develop Your Latent Paranormal Powers

put your hands (palm to palm), together, tightly and firmly. Both of you are to now close your eyes. You must imagine a white static-like light moving slowly down your arm. From your shoulders to your hands. The white light should look like a giant electric spark. You must imagine this white light flowing easily through your arms, hands, and finally, through your fingertips. You should now be able to see it flowing into the other person's hands. You must feel this energy. If you can imagine seeing it, then you should be able to get yourself to also feel it.   While you are imagining it flowing into the other person's hands, from your hands, you can slowly pull your hands away. But make sure to keep them facing palm to palm with the other person's hands. You should still be mentally commanding the power flowing into the other person's hands – only it will have greater distance to travel from your hands to hers/his. After you have a fine image of it flowing from your hand, through the distance of air into the other person's hands. You can slowly start moving your hands so your fingertips are facing that person's hands, but your palms are facing down.

After you have a firm image of the electricity flowing from your hands into your friend's hands, you can slowly bend each finger into your palm, so that you finally end up with just your index finger (pointing finger), pointing at the other person's palm.   After you have a firm image (you still need to be able to feel the energy flowing), try moving your finger in a circle, putting your finger closer, then further away, from the palm of the other person's hand. The other person should feel tingling as you do this. Every time you make a change in how your hand is facing, or moving, the other person should be able to feel it as it changes.   When you have done this for a couple weeks with a person (only with one person at a time), you can try this with two people. In other words your right hand is palm to palm with one person, and your left hand is palm to palm with another person. The time will soon come when everyone in your group has learned energy weaving with one or two people. You now have a circle of people who can energy weave. This circle now has the power to continue to the next step.

Practice for several weeks and when you feel that you are ready, you and another person can now try energy weaving with something in-between the two of you. Try something small at first, a book, a metal object, a small flat stone. You both should be touching the object the entire time.   It is recommended that you use a metal object, glass, or a clear natural crystal at first because these objects will enhance the energy flow, and you will not only be able to feel the energy in your hands, but in the object as well. You actually end up charging the object with your personal power/powers by doing this.

This energy can now be channeled and used in all sorts of interesting ways. Try moving a small object like a button or bottle cap. It is really very easy once you learn to control your energies and focus them properly.

Develop Your Latent Paranormal Powers

Telekinesis (TK), often called psychokinesis, is basically the ability to move an object on the physical position using only psychic power, which means using your thoughts and energies to control objects.

The famous psychic Uri Geller can stop watches and bend spoons using only his paranormal powers to control the objects. He discovered his powers when he was around five. One day during a meal, his spoon curled up in his hand, although he had not applied any physical force. From this start Uri Geller learned to control and channel his energies to open up a fantastic range of psychic abilities. You may not be as successful as Uri Geller, but you will be amazed at what you can do once you set your mind to it.

There are many things you can do with telekinesis, we are all born with this skill but most of us never learn to use this amazing ability properly. What you can do to help you along the way is have an accepting attitude. Believe it can happen. Everyone ever taught this technique who was successful in moving and controlling objects, had a positive attitude. They may not have believed they could do it but they did believe it was possible. That's a start for the proper frame of mind.

Focus your attention. So many people say they are concentrating but in fact their minds are scattered and they aren't really into it at all. Be there. Learn to do only one thing at a time. Practice being still. Yes, actually, being still without thinking anything. Try it. All the masters have acquired this skill. They can actually, sit still and think of nothing. This is why they are able to control their paranormal powers.

They know how not to cause ripples in the universal energy. Opening a lock with the wave of a hand, or walking about seemingly invisible, traveling from place to place in the blink of an eye, even levitation. They have mastered the Self. They truly can focus on one thing and only one thing at a time. The longer you can sit still and still your mind, the more available energy you have. It is in that discipline that teaches, patience, acceptance and unconditional being. This is a skill that will enhance every aspect of your life.

Remember, when you think on something it will attract like thoughts. Twenty seconds of one pure thought attracts an equal amount of pure energy of the same resonance and quality. Each twenty mark increases a multiplies the energy. Can you imagine what you could manifest just by two minutes of pure unadulterated thought? This equation works equally for both types of thoughts – be they positive or negative in origin. Be mindful of what you think about. Every action you take was proceeded by a thought. What was the quality of yours? Those were some of the techniques that will help you open up to all your abilities.

Develop Your Latent Paranormal Powers

Using Telekinesis To Move An Object

Choose a small object, preferably made of a light metal, such as a cheap ring or an earring. Concentration is the most important factor – and visualization is the second most vital thing. Clear your mind completely. You should have no distractions, and try not to let bothersome thoughts into your mind, or you will lose your focus.

Once you feel you are ready, build a "tunnel" between you and the object – this visualization will help you to focus on the object alone, and not the distractions "outside the tunnel."

Now, imagine your mind's hands coming out and pulling the object towards you using your energy weaving and "human magnetism." Don't expect this to work the first time you try it. It might, but more than likely it will not. Practice makes perfect so try, try again. A very important thing is to remember that it is possible, it has been done and can be done again. Your outlook on the possibility will affect your success, and ultimately, make the experience worthwhile. If you want to hurl an object at someone or something basically think on who or what you want to hit. also you have to have a lot of energy for this, and a lot of patience. If you've had experiences with telekinesis before and want to control it, think of the mood you had before you moved it and try to put yourself into this mood again, this might help.

Do this for as long as you're comfortable, and do it daily. After some time you will start to see results. Light things are easiest, so start light. Rolling a pen or a small ball by touching it less each time, making a toothpick in a glass of water float in the direction you want, trying to make the fire of a candle lean to one direction and then another, balancing a spoon on the edge of a glass and trying to make the spoon rock off, and bending silverware or keys.

Bending silverware is a little different. You hold the choice object in your hand, and you feel the surface as you imagine in your head bending the silverware. The thing is, you don't "make" it bend, you "let" it bend. Levitation is pretty much a form of telekinesis so use the same method as telekinesis if you want to levitate something or yourself off the ground.

Your Paranormal Wishing Device

If you have ever wanted a particular wish or desire to come true, but had trouble focusing your energies on this desire, here is a very simple, but amazingly powerful device that will help you focus your thoughts like a laser beam of energy.

First you need to write down just what it is you want. Do you need more money? Do you want a new and better job? Are you interested in someone and want them to

Develop Your Latent Paranormal Powers

be interested in you? Whatever it is you want, write it down. Keep your request short and to the point. "I will have more money!" "I will get a new and better job!" "I will attract the attention of the one I love." Don't write it down as a wish, make a power statement: "I will get my desire!"

Now take a regular sheet of white paper and roll it into a cone. Make sure the small end is left open to about an inch in diameter. You will need to see through this opening, so leave some room. Tape it together so it retains its shape.

Next you need to shape your energy into a compact ball of power. You cup your hands as if holding something between them, and then visualize yourself as a conduit of universal energy, and just let it flow out through your hands and into a ball between them. Imagine this ball of energy as white-hot and bursting with the paranormal energy that is needed to make your wish come true. You can tell if you are successful by paying attention to your hands. They will get hot and your hand will have little twitches every now and then.

When you have built the energy up to as high as you think you need, take your power cone and paper with your wish written on it – point the small end of the cone at your wish and visualize your ball of power entering the large end and being concentrated into a shaft of laser light. Read each word you have written down through the small end of the cone. Imagine the laser energy burning each word with its paranormal powers. It is important that you keep your mind focused on the task at hand. You have accumulated a vast amount of power for your goal. Don't waste it on stray thoughts. Keep your one wish in mind at all times.

Continue to illuminate each word of your wish until you have run out of power. At that point, stop for the day. You can try again in 24 hours. Allow enough time for your batteries to recharge. This is a very powerful technique, so don't be fooled by how simple it seems. Because of this, make sure that your wish is something you really want. As the old saying goes: "Be careful what you wish for, because it just may come true."

You can also use this technique to influence the thoughts of others. Practice with a friend. Write one word down and build your energy ball. Using your cone of power, try and project your word to the mind of your friend. Imagine the laser light burning the word into energy and transmitting it across the distance to your friend. You'll be amazed how easy this works.

After awhile, you can learn to influence the thoughts of others by using your paranormal powers. The next time you are at a party or in the mall, practice this technique on someone who is seated nearby. As before, visualize your energy ball and with your mind, turn it into a shaft of powerful laser light. Take five deep breaths and quickly exhale them, don't hold them in. Choose someone who is nearby and has their back towards you.

Develop Your Latent Paranormal Powers

Concentrate your laser beam onto the back of the head of your test subject. Don't stare, just keep your attention focused on this person. See the white beam of light leaving your body and entering the head of your test subject. You will soon see that this person will start to fidget and look around. Soon they will turn and look right in your direction. Success! You are on your way to developing your paranormal abilities to influence the thoughts of others.

Continue to practice this technique with your friends. (Don't tell them what you are doing however, as this will set up a psychic block that will be hard to break through.) Now, instead of just sending a laser beam, send a thought or command in this energy to the mind of your practice subject. Tell them to scratch their head, or get up to get a drink. Start simple and build on your successes.

Use this ability wisely, don't abuse your power. The universe has a way of preventing people from taking unfair advantage of others, so don't waste your powers to cause harm. This paranormal potential manifests itself in many ways. Sometimes when we have to make decisions or take some form of action we know exactly what to do, but at other times and on similar circumstances we are not so sure of what action to take. People who always seem to be in the right place at the right time, and for whom good things happen with uncanny frequency, are not just plain lucky – they have an intuitive sense of choosing, deciding and how to act to a given situation. Intuitive revelations steer the course for man to discover and invent and creative talents to originate.

Developing your paranormal powers can be accomplished if you know when you are psychically active. You can then use this knowledge to react to current events and know what action to take immediately, what to delay to a better cyclical period. You will intuitively know what to do or not do when you know what days are likely to produce failure and what days are likely to produce success.

If you are one who is a reject of success, one who has tried and tried and failed and has accepted the existence that fate has handed you – don't despair, try again. Follow your heart and rekindle the flame which will lead you to successes beyond your dreams.

Our lives were meant to be lived and enjoyed to their fullest. But usually we become so caught up in the everyday trivialities of day-to-day living that we lose sight of what is really important. Most of us go about our daily lives in a sort of stupor. We live like robots that have been programmed to perform the same functions day after day with no deviation from the program. We are asleep at the wheel with no desire to awaken and take control.

This is no way to live. Every day should be a new and different experience and we should greet it with the same excitement and expectations as a child greets Christmas morning or a trip to their favorite amusement park. We must shake

Develop Your Latent Paranormal Powers

ourselves awake and look about at the wonderful universe that we helped create and acknowledge how important a role we play.

Easier said than done? We do live in the material world and must obey the laws of reality. However, does this mean that we must forever live as slaves to the dull parameters of the robot and the solid fabric of existence? Is there more to our bleak lives than the constant ticking away of the seconds and minutes bringing us ever closer to death and decay? Can we finally break the stranglehold of mere mindless existence to allow our spirits to soar with the eagles on the celestial winds of creation?

One of the simplest facts concerning our place in this world is also the hardest to accept: We have complete control over our lives. It is as simple as that. However, this seems to be in direct contrast to our daily experiences which seem to show that we have about as much control of our lives as a leaf has while caught up in a windstorm. We feel helpless as our lives are blown helter-skelter about by the seemingly uncaring universe. The more helpless we feel, the more out of control our lives becomes. It is a wonder that we are able to endure at all in this chaotic world.

This is where the robot comes in. We learn early on that if we maintain the same patterns day after day we can just squeak by with life. Unfortunately this way of living leaves us with little real opportunity and unable to cope when the universe gives us a gentle shove in different directions. The robot is incapable of dealing with new and different situations and in the process of maintaining the old ways, flounders about making things even worse.

Are you a robot? How do you deal with life when you come across an obstacle? Can you look beyond your programming to see the different paths that are placed in front of you, or do you blindly strive to keep the status quo no matter what the final outcome? If you are tired of stumbling about in the darkness that has become your life, now is the time to change your life path and seize what the universe has freely made available to us all.

Cruise The Universe With Your Astral Body

The sensation of having an existence separate from one's physical body, and even being able to stand outside of oneself is a strange but common paranormal experience. Out of body experiences (OOBEs) cannot be dismissed as mere hallucination or fantasy, because often a person has been seen by others while traveling in his or her astral body. Sometimes the cosmic traveler has acquired information from a physically remote location thereby proving that the experience was real.

Develop Your Latent Paranormal Powers

It is easy to learn how to travel the astral planes of existence. There are a number of methods available for your experimentation. However, you will find that only one or two methods work best for you. It is advisable for you to try several methods to find which works for you. Here are a couple of methods that most people find easy to work.

Step 1. - Before dropping off to sleep, put your body into a deep state of relaxation. Do this by systematically tensing and relaxing each muscle one at a time. Start with the toes and work up the body to the face. This will put your body into such an unfamiliar deep state of relaxation that in the early days you may feel a little discomfort. Your body may feel unbearably heavy but there's nothing to worry about.

Step 2. - Now let your breathing become slow and deep. Slow, deep breathing will relax you further and keep you alert. Focus your attention on the center of your forehead but don't fall asleep.

Step 3. - Become aware of just how heavy your body feels. Think of it as being cumbersome and made of clay. Now set your attention on your astral duplicate body. See it as made of light. It is weightless and free. Picture in your mind's eye images of bubbles, sunlight, feathers floating on the breeze, smoke rising upwards. Your body is heavy but your soul is weightless.

Step 4. - At this point many people report of being able to 'see' the darkened room even though their eyes are closed. It appears to be bathed in a purple light. If you get this far, try to focus your attention on the ceiling light fitting.

Step 5. - Imagine drawing the light bulb towards you. As you do this you may feel yourself floating towards the ceiling. Try to remain conscious. You will become aware of floating in your astral self and may even see your sleeping body laid below you on the bed.

Another good method is called **The Moving Anchor**. After meditating into a state of total deep relaxation, imagine an object about six feet in front of your eyes. Now feel this object pulling at you like a magnet. Once you can see the object clearly in your mind's eye and feel the pull of the object on you, begin to move the object slowly towards you. Just a small amount at first. As the object moves towards you feel the pull getting stronger. Now move it back again (the pull gets weaker as you do). Now repeat the process moving the object closer each time and feeling the pull becoming stronger and stronger as the object comes closer.

Once you are comfortable with the movement of the object begin the process again, only this time the movement of the object should be a fluid motion, and as the object moves to and fro it should be like a wave. You should also feel this wave on yourself as the pull gets stronger and weaker and stronger again. Finally as the

Develop Your Latent Paranormal Powers

object virtually reaches you the strength of the pulling force combined with the wave like motion will simply pull you right out of your physical body.

One more excellent and easy method is to simply lay down with the lights off. Make sure you are completely relaxed. Lie there and be quite and still, calm and clear your mind. Imagine your astral body which may look like grey matter shaped in the form of your body. Imagine it lifting and floating out of your body, floating up to the ceiling in your room. Turn and look down and try to see you body lying there. If you are successful you may want to stay in the room and float around a bit, staying close to the body. Or you can choose to walk through walls and travel to where ever you wish to go. You can fly there or you can will yourself there instantly.

Just remember when trying to astral project: You need to be calm and very relaxed. You should not be over full in the stomach or feeling hungry. Practice only when your mind can be focused. Make sure the room temperature is comfortable. Do not get too excited or fired up. Stay balanced. People who are having relationship problems usually have difficulty in projecting.

The Wonders Of Time Travel

Time, with its relentless passageway through our lives, appears impossible to conquer or even tame. Yet, despite the overwhelming odds against it, we all have the innate desire to change our past and know our future. It is as if we know, deep-down within the core of our souls, that time is not so insurmountable after all. That time as we know it, does not really exist.

For your astral self, time travel is real and possible. When you project your astral body you can journey into the past, present or future, and come back whenever you are ready. This easy method will take you through time by means of the astral planes and visualization. Your physical body will remain safe at home – it is your astral self that will travel and interact with time. Some people, after mastering astral time travel, have reported that they have learned to send their physical body across time and space. However, this is a feat that should not be attempted by the novice. Reports of people mysteriously disappearing forever could be the result of accidental activation of this time-bending ability.

Before you start, practice your favorite meditation technique. If you cannot meditate then you will have no success with this type of time travel. You must be able to go into your meditative state and clear your mind of all outside thoughts and distractions. This is an exercise that is best done in private. Please make sure that you can practice in a quiet room absent of any bother.

As you meditate, imagine a building in the middle of a field or in the middle of

Develop Your Latent Paranormal Powers

nowhere surrounded by nothing. You will use this same building every time you practice. The building can be any shape or size. Many imagine their very own pyramid. Your building should have no windows, this way you will not be disturbed by anything on the "outside." The inside of this building can be as simple or as plush as you wish it to be. The simpler it is, however, the fewer distractions you will have. Just make sure it is the same every time you practice.

Imagine that inside this building will be a room where you have a chair. This chair, a big black recliner with controls built into the arm, is a special chair. These controls are buttons that will take you where you want to go. You may set up these buttons in any configuration. For instance – a past button – a present button – and a future button. For even more control, try a LED display with a number key pad for punching in the exact year in time you wish to travel. If you do not want to use a chair, you may imagine some big elaborate machine with all the same controls.

In this room will also be a giant movie screen. This screen is where you will be watching the time frame you have chosen. Try to think of how you want all these items – the building – the time machine – the screen – before you actually go into meditation. Predetermine how you want them all to look beforehand.

Go into your meditative state. When you are totally relaxed take a mental walk to your special building and close the door. Sit in your special chair or machine and relax for a few more minutes.

When you are ready, push the button that makes your screen come down from the ceiling and just sit there and stare at it for a minute. Now, dial in what time period and where you travel. Do not try to force this to happen, you must remain patient for the screen to come on. If you are impatient, it will not happen. Your mind must be receptive to what is being shown. It may take several days of trying before you actually see anything but, it will happen.

When you want to come back... just push the buttons for the present on your chair and take a few minutes to evaluate everything you saw. then when you are ready get up out of your chair and walk out of the building and back to your physical body.

As you practice this method, you will soon find that you no longer need the building, the time machine or the screen. These are mental constructions to help you learn how it "feels" to travel through time. Once you have learned how to do this, you can travel back and forth through time as effortlessly as going to sleep at night.

As you travel through time, you can actually take part again in your past triumphs and attempt to fix your mistakes and failures. You can even see the possible realities that are created by your efforts. You can even travel to and occupy one of these other realities for as short or as long as you want. It makes no difference because you can return to your body seconds after you left. Time has no meaning to the astral plane.

Develop Your Latent Paranormal Powers

This method can also be used to have the Ascended Masters show you things you need to learn. Just go through the same process and ask the Masters to show you on the screen what you want to know.

Another method that is very popular with students of the paranormal is to lie back on your bed in a comfortable position, gently close your eyes and relax. Letting go of any pain take slow, deep comfortable breaths through the nose.

Without worry or fear, clear your mind of distracting thoughts. You can focus on your breath or chant a favorite mantra. Imagine you're in an elevator moving upwards. Vividly feel the upwards motion.

Now relax completely to that point between sleep and consciousness, keep focused on the image and feeling of moving up. Tell yourself you will wake up fully out of the body. Imagine you are rising up from your body and drift off to sleep.

To move in time: Focus very vividly on the time you want to journey. Feel what is happening at that very moment. You will experience the feeling of moving very rapidly through the air. Some report the feeling of moving through water or very dense gas. You may catch glimpses of your past and future as you travel. Stay focused on where you want to go. The slightest distraction will send you off into a completely different direction.

When you arrive at your destination, you may have trouble focusing on what is going on around you. This is often reported by first-timers to the world of time travel. The sensations that you are now able to perceive can be overwhelming and even frightening. Not only will you be aware of your own feelings and thoughts, you will also be aware of what everyone else is thinking as well. When the sensations become too intense, it is time for you to return to try again some other time.

When you have learned that time is meaningless to you – you are free to travel when and wherever you want in this universe. However, with this ability comes great responsibility. If your purpose is to try and change the past, you should realize that changing the past could affect your present situation for the worse. Most often, on your return, nothing will seem to have happened. Other times you will find yourself in a present that is completely different from the world you left. This is because with every change of your past, new and different realities are created. You may find yourself occupying a new world with no desire to return to the world that you left behind.

The Amazing Powers of Visualization

Would you like to experience your personal best? To feel confident, secure, competent, poised and self-assured? Would you like to look and feel your "ideal"

Develop Your Latent Paranormal Powers

self? Would you perhaps like to work at a fulfilling job that utilizes your talents and rewards you financially?

Would you like to control your own future and have command of amazing powers of the mind?

Most of us would answer a resounding "Yes!" to at least some of the above questions. But too few of us know how to make these ideals a part of our lives. We too often feel out of control, not competent or confident about our goal; we often don't know how or where to start. If we only realized that it is easy to start and it is easy to know how – once we gain a clear vision of what we want.

Vision is the catalyst that jump starts all change that lights the way toward all growth. Without vision, goals and ideals are merely unrealized dreams. Vision is that clear, constant image of what we want and where we are going that we hold in our minds. Visualization is the mind tool that you can use to create that vision.

Visualization is the process of creating vision, and that process is simple; it can be learned and used by anyone. Visualization works because it creates belief, belief that can alter the circumstances of your life. Visualization literally means creating pictures in your mind. With visualization, you speak directly to your subconscious mind, by-passing the censorship of the logical, conscious mind. Your subconscious mind thinks in pictures, and you can reach the programming levels of your subconscious mind quickly and easily with visualization. Visualization is an idea, a thought form, in picture.

By starting with a picture, you take a short-cut directly into your subconscious. No words have to be translated from conscious (left-brain) language to subconscious (right-brain) language. You deliver a simple, clear, direct message right into your subconscious mind. Creating visualizations of the things you want to believe is very effective. Your subconscious mind does not rationalize. It takes whatever you give it as truth. If you consistently picture yourself as having already achieved your goal, your subconscious mind soon believes that it is so. Then, in order to balance your inner and outer reality, your subconscious sets into motion any events or circumstances necessary to create in the physical realm that which you believe in your mind to be true.

Visualization is a bit of mental trickery. You are, in effect, tricking your subconscious into believing that an event has occurred when it has not. This is where visualization can help. "Seeing is believing" for most people. We believe what we see with our own eyes. The same holds true for mental seeing.

Visualizing a scene in your mind tends to make it more real. You come to believe in the reality of the image. At first visualization of a goal may seem forced and unnatural. But repeated visualizations, like repeated affirmations, slowly create the belief that the desired goal is possible, then probable, then, finally, a fact. And once a

Develop Your Latent Paranormal Powers

goal has become real in your mind, once you believe it, it starts to become real in your life.

Using affirmations (positive statements that we repeat to ourselves in a positive way) and visualization together is like a "double whammy" for creating belief in your desired goal. One or the other alone will work, but by using the two together, your success will come easier and faster.

Visualize your desired goal while you repeat your affirmation for it. Create a scene in your mind where you see yourself already having achieved your goal. See yourself doing what you would be doing, saying what you would be saying, feeling what you would be feeling. By making your visualization vivid, active and exciting, you add energy to it.

Visualize Your Reality

Close your eyes and imagine a movie or television screen about six inches away from your face and up a couple inches above your eyes. This is where you should make your mental pictures. You do not need to get the exact details, (most people don't really see details like hair and eyes on their figures). In fact, when you see an image or visualization, it is in the form of a thought-picture, a sort of mix between an actual image and just the thought of that image.

Don't expect pictures like those on television. Trying too hard to get a good visualization will hamper your results. Sometimes you sense an image more than you actually see it.

It is a good idea to create a time every day to mentally send out your visualized goals. Often people do it just before they fall off to sleep. Another good time is shortly after awakening in the morning, before you start your day. You can add energy to your visualizations by accompanying them with affirmations, or positive statements that also reflect your goal.

Here are some excellent examples of creative visualization – you can use these to help create your own methods that will work best for your own unique circumstances.

Visualizations For Prosperity And Success – Picture yourself experiencing your prosperity and wealth. What kinds of possessions would you have? What would your bank statement look like? Visualize yourself using and enjoying your prosperity. Also, and this is very important, visualize the good that will come from your increased prosperity. What positive ways will you use your money? Picture your success in specific, positive images. See yourself performing a service of your choice that others need and appreciate. See yourself being congratulated and praised for your good work. Imagine that you have a never-ending supply of people who value and want your services. See yourself enjoying your work, feeling proud and happy that you can provide this worthwhile service.

If you are not happy with your present job, see yourself working and doing the kinds of things you would really like to be doing. Imagine yourself in the type of environment you feel best – at home, at an office, outside, a wonderful job (and you do not have to know exactly what this job is – you can leave that up to the universe).

See yourself depositing a paycheck into your bank account. This check shows the amount of money that you need and desire from your work. Perhaps you have plans to help others in some way. Visualize this happening. Any time you use your increased prosperity to help others, you increase your potential for prosperity becoming a permanent part of your life.

Your attitude about prosperity and plenty increases your wealth. Think of money as freedom, as a tool to help you do what you do best. Perhaps there is a special job or some volunteer work that you have been wanting to do, but never got around to.

Use your prosperity wisely, and more will come to you. Think of your wealth as freedom, security, and added power to help others. When you want to create prosperity, attitude is everything.

Visualizations For Health – Picture yourself on your mental screen, seeing yourself at your healthy best. Imagine yourself strong, vital and healthy as you make your health affirmations. If there are any areas in your body that need attention, imagine each area specifically, seeing it whole, complete and healed of whatever ailment it once had. Make an affirmation that the ailment is now healed. You might imagine a healing light permeating every cell of the affected area. Then, see yourself joyfully experiencing freedom from this ailment. Move the body part freely, breathe deeply, whatever, to show that the body part is no longer affected.

End the visualization by giving thanks for your perfect health. You can also do these visualizations for others, imaging them on your mental screen.

Visualizations For Happiness – Imagine the kinds of things that you want and need to be truly happy in your life. Affirm that you have these. Visualize a peaceful scene where your best wishes have come true. Give thanks for the happiness in your life.

There are unlimited ways to visualize. Make your visualizations unique and real according to your own desires. Always remember to visualize the positive outcome of your goal. Visualize the good that will result from having achieved your goal. Visualize yourself appreciative and thankful. The universe likes to be thanked.

Visualizations For Emotional Healing – Not only can you program goals and desires with your visualizations, you can re-program old hurts and change old non-productive, limiting attitudes. If you are committed to looking deeply and

Develop Your Latent Paranormal Powers

openly into your own mind, using visualization for emotional healing is something that you can do alone. For most people, however, visualization can be a real tool in helping them uncover and re-program their own
mental patterns. There are several visualizations that you can use to speak directly to your subconscious and re-program those patterns that are not helpful to you in your present life.

One method called the ***Small Child Visualization***, developed by Rita Milios, is especially good for re-programming very old beliefs and attitudes. In it you meet yourself as you were when you were a child. You then go back to an old feeling or problem and mentally visualize its solution by you the adult, taking the child's problem and mentally releasing it.

A good releasing image is to visualize the problem being dissolved by a bright, golden sun, or to see your adult self placing the problem in a hot air balloon and letting it float away. Even if you don't know the exact problem, by tapping into anxieties, fears or negative feelings, you can still get in touch with the mental program associated with those feelings and release it.

You may want to go through this visualization several times, each time dealing with a new problem or feeling. An especially difficult problem may take several repeated visualizations to clear out all of the negative energy associated with the original mental program. Just follow your intuitive feelings. They will tell you when you have repeated a visualization enough times. You will know also if a sense of peace comes over you during the visualization, or you experience the cessation of a specific anxiety.

Visualization is a continuing process. It can be made better with practice. Creating your own vivid scenes is the key to using visualization. Practice these simple exercises until you become a natural at visualization. It can be honed to perfection. The better you become at visualization, the more creative energy you will have available to you to create your desired reality.

Creative Energy

Physicist Max Planck found that photons (units of light energy) acted as either particles or as waves, depending on the experimenter's intent. When a photon is placed in an experiment designed to show that it acts as a wave, it will. And when the photon is placed in an experiment designed to show that it acts as a particle, it stops acting like a wave and starts acting like a particle. In either case, Planck's intent did not simply interfere with the energy's movement; instead it dominated what the energy "chose" to do.

Develop Your Latent Paranormal Powers

Planck's findings have enormous implications. Since he showed that the behavior of energy is influenced by the intent of the observer, the implication is that you can intentionally impact how your creative energy acts. How you look and feel about certain events will have influence on them. Your creative energy will transform those events.

In another experiment, but in the field of psychology, Joseph Banks Rhine found that intention influences matter. His research, which took place in the Parapsychology Laboratory of North Carolina's Duke University, focused on the ability of a person to will the outcome of a dice roll.

Through his extensive and thorough research, Rhine determined that a definite relationship exists beyond the margin of chance between the intention of the person casting the dice and the outcome of the roll. What could explain Rhine's findings? Could the dice's energy have been influenced by the intention of the person tossing the dice? Hypothetically, yes. Like Planck's photons, Rhine's dice behaved as if influenced by the intent of their observer.

In everyday terms this means that, if you want to have control over what your energy creates, you must maintain awareness of your thoughts and intentions. If you expect to see yourself cheated, your energy will transform itself to create experiences in which you are cheated. Likewise, if you expect to see yourself winning, your energy will transform itself to create winning experiences. Still, one has to wonder: How does your energy know what to do? How does it know what you think?

Further experimentation in quantum physics makes it clear that photons somehow process information and therefore appear to have awareness. In the book, ***Schrodinger's Kittens and the Search for Reality***, John Gribbin writes of an experiment which showed that when a flow of photons faced a two-slit passageway, the photons acted wave-like, heading for both entrances. When the experimenter suddenly decreased the passageway to one slit, the photon flow became particle-like with the photons flowing in a bee-line straight toward the single slit. Because no photons attempted to enter the missing slit, physicists were left with the question: How did the photons "know" that there was only one slit through which to travel?

While physicists continue to grapple with the implications of this experiment, the evidence points to the phenomenon that photons have some type of awareness that allows them to know what to do. Consequently it can be assumed (though it has yet to be explained how or why) that awareness and "knowingness" exist at the energy level.

In addition, an Einstein, Podolsky, and Rosen (also known as EPR) thought experiment addressed the hypothesis that subatomic particles actually communicate with each other (see: ***Teleportation: From Star Trek to Tesla*** by Commander X and Tim Swartz - Global Communications). They knew that a two-particle system of zero spin behaves in a certain way: when set in motion (traveling at the speed of light), one particle always spins in the polar opposite direction from its mate.

Therefore, if particle A is spinning upward, particle B will spin downward. If A spins to the left, B will spin to the right. The EPR experiment eventually showed that if, after the particles are set in motion, the experimenter magnetically changes the direction of one particle, its mate would also change its direction. Thus, if A is initially moving to the right at the speed of light and spinning on an upward axis, B will be moving to the left at the speed of light and spinning on a downward axis. When the experimenter magnetically distorts A's axis so that it spins to the left, B instantly changes its axis so that it spins to the right, even though the particles are going in opposite directions at the speed of light.

How does B know what is happening to A? While it may seem unfathomable, Einstein, Podolsky, and Rosen's experiment illustrates that energy particles communicate with each other in an indiscernible, unrecognizable way.

Both these experiments demonstrate that units of energy have a type of awareness and that they communicate with each other, though perhaps not in the same ways humans or other living things are aware and communicate.

Humans, for example, process thought through their brains, which energy particles apparently do not have. These experiments imply that our energy too has awareness and can communicate; our energy can know what we want and can communicate this to the energy of the universe that exists outside and within ourselves.

Energy Is The Presence of Thought

According to the mystic and philosopher Mintanyo, energy is actually the presence of thought. Thought is the activating component of all that is. Thought, in the nothingness, is a force, much like gravitational or magnetic force; it hovers, shimmers, and shivers until the nothingness actually takes on or absorbs the movement.

Nothingness that is moving is what we perceive to be energy. Energy is actually the movement of thought. This energy in turn is absorbed by mass. Therefore, you can say that thought energizes the nothingness into **somethingness**, and that somethingness is basically absorbed thought. This means that energy is actually thought.

The universe, our reality, is thought made real. As each thought is thought, a part of the nothingness is moved by it. This movement is what we call energy. Thus, when we say that energy is absorbed, what we are really saying is the thought is

Develop Your Latent Paranormal Powers

absorbed. And each time a particle of thought is absorbed by an atom, then a molecule, and so on, the thought becomes a part of the atom, then the molecule, and so on. As a result, we can assume that everything around us to some extent absorbs our thoughts, just as we to some extent absorb the thoughts of everything else. Bearing this in mind, it is no wonder that scientists have detected that energy responds to thought and intent.

In real life, this transformation of thought into a state of energy and then into a state of mass may translate into an experience. Each time we focus on an idea or goal, the thought instantly becomes energy, creative energy, which is subsequently absorbed by atoms and molecules; eventually it becomes part of a thing which emulates the thought. Obviously the more prevalent our thoughts, the more creative energy produced. In addition, creative energy interacts and communicates with other energy particles, which then begin to take part in becoming the thing that is thought.

Your ego and your creative energy function together as a system to create your life experiences. Your ego holds your beliefs, which it keeps alive on a continual basis, and your creative energy transforms itself into experiences which reflect the beliefs. This is why it is said that your experiences mirror your beliefs.

Remaining aware that your ego and creative energy function together as a system is useful because it implies that it will alert you when it cannot create the positive experiences you really want to have. This allows you the opportunity to give it what it needs to create beneficial, rather than negative, experiences.

Unleash Your Psychic Powers With Meditation

Meditation is one of the simplest tools you can use to help you tune into your natural psychic ability. It requires no belief or lifestyle change, is non-religious, is not time-consuming, and can be learned by anyone regardless of age or level of education. The transformation people often experience once they learn to meditate, and make it a regular practice in their lives, is to return to their natural state of being. Yes, this quiet little practice can in fact change your life.

Meditation is a process of moving from the scattered, unfocused state of our everyday consciousness to a state of consciousness that brings serenity, clarity, and bliss. Constant thought-activity, especially of random nature, can tire the mind and even bring on headaches. Meditation attempts to transcend this rather chaotic level of thought activity. Through meditation we learn to calm and control our thoughts bringing a greater sense of purpose to that which we want achieved.

Develop Your Latent Paranormal Powers

Meditation involves concentrating on something to take our attention beyond the scattered thought activity that is usually going on in our heads. This can involve a solid object or picture, a mantra, breath, or guided visualization.

Typical objects employed include a candle flame or a flower. Some people use pictures, such as a mandala – a highly colored symmetric painting – or a picture of a spiritual teacher. Mantras are sounds which have a flowing, meditative quality and may be repeated out loud or inwardly. The breath is also a common focal point. Finally, guided visualization is also considered by some to be a form of meditation. A guided visualization can help to bring one into a meditative state; also, visualization may be used once a meditative state has been reached to produce various results.

Learning to meditate is really very simple. There is no "wrong" way to meditate. You may have to try several different techniques in order to find what works best with you, but you will soon find the method that resonates with your inner self. Just remember that you shouldn't try to force something to happen. Just let it happen on its own. Nor should you try to make your mind blank or chase thoughts away.

Often we experience sensations in meditation: emotions, feelings of changing size and shape, delight, awe, fear and so on. These are different for everyone, and are part of your own path. Allow yourself to witness and learn from the experience, but don't try or expect to repeat it, or to understand the experience. Accept what is there, ask for nothing and appreciate what is happening.

Pick a focus word or short phrase that's firmly rooted in your personal belief system. A nonreligious person might choose a neutral word like one, peace, or love. Others might use the opening words of a favorite prayer from their religion. "OM" is very popular because of the soothing body resonance produced by the word.

Find a quiet, comfortable place to meditate. You can sit in a comfortable chair, on the bed, on the floor – anywhere that's comfortable. Eliminate as much noise and as many potential distractions as possible. Don't worry about those things that you can not control.

When you sit to meditate, sit comfortably, with your spine reasonably straight. This allows the life force energy to flow freely up the spine, which is an important aspect of meditation. Leaning against a chair back, a wall, headboard, etc. is perfectly all right. If, for physical reasons, you can't sit up, lay flat on your back. Place your hands in any position that is comfortable.

If it does not go against your beliefs, call on a "higher source" for assistance in your meditation. This can be very helpful, but it is not absolutely necessary. Commit yourself to a specific length of time and try to stick to it.

Breathing is very important to achieve the proper meditative state. Focusing on breathing is a wonderful way to revitalize ourselves on many levels. It is also a simple technique for calming and focusing the awareness. For beginners, it a simple

Develop Your Latent Paranormal Powers

practice which can be done at any time, and is for this reason is a great place to start in learning to meditate.

Sit in a comfortable, quiet place with your spine relatively straight to allow the free flow of life force through your breath. Close your eyes, or if you prefer, sit with your eyes slightly open and gazing downward. If you wish, place the tip of your tongue on the roof of your mouth, just behind the teeth.

Take a few moments to allow your breath to become calm and regular, but don't force it, allow it to take it's natural pace in and out of your body. Place your hand, palm facing downwards on your stomach. Gently breathe in and feel your hand being pushed outwards as your intake of air fills your diaphragm – to a gentle slow count of 1...2...3...4... As you breathe in, feel it rising up the front of your body, reaching the top of your head as your lungs fill completely.

Hold your breath – without straining – to a gentle slow count of 1... 2... 3...4... Exhale slowly to the same count of 1... 2... 3... 4...as you exhale, feel the breath cascading down the back of your body, reaching your toes as you release the last of your breath. Finally hold again for 1... 2... 3... 4... Continue to breathe in and out with awareness of your breath in this manner for as long as you are able. If a thought intrudes, gently guide the attention back to your breath. Do not try to push the thought away, but simply return attention to your breath.

Relax your muscles sequentially from head to feet. This helps to break the connection between stressful thoughts and a tense body. Starting with your forehead, become aware of tension as you breathe in. Let go of any obvious tension as you breathe out. Go through the rest of your body in this way, proceeding down through your eyes, jaws, neck, shoulders, arms, hands, chest, upper back, middle back and midriff, lower back, belly, pelvis, buttocks, thighs, calves, and feet.

Breathe slowly and naturally, repeating your focus word or phrase silently as you exhale. Assume a passive attitude. Don't worry about how well you're doing. When other thoughts come to mind, simply say, "Oh, well," and gently return to the repetition.

Continue for 10 to 20 minutes. You may open your eyes to check the time, but do not use an alarm. After you finish: Sit quietly for a minute or so, at first with your eyes closed and later with your eyes open. Do not stand for one or two minutes.

You will soon find that with meditation, your mind becomes more receptive to the universal energies that flow through us. This energy is the creative force that can be controlled and used by proper thought.

XXX

Develop Your Latent Paranormal Powers

Getting What You Really Want

With all the self-help information available today, why isn't everybody happy and why doesn't everyone get what they want. Why are so many people struggling to achieve something only to give up in frustration? How many self-help or motivational workshops have you attended only to have the excitement wear off after a short period of time?

What do you think an individual really believes who affirms 50 times a day. "I'm rich. I'm rich. I'm rich." You guessed it, he really believes that he is not rich. He is also strengthening the thought form that is already keeping him from being rich. He'll soon see no results for his efforts and give up in frustration.

His limiting belief could have to do with money but my guess is that is has to do with a personal belief, such as not deserving it or something related to that. What's required for permanent change in your experience is a shift in focus from trying to overpower old beliefs with new ones, to a focus on identifying and simply dissolving the old beliefs that no longer serve you.

There are numerous self-development books, tapes and workshops available – all with good intent and of useful benefit. In many cases though, the benefit is temporary. There is a good reason for this. Many techniques don't address the cause of your experience. They try to implement new techniques that focus on overpowering or going around the old situation to create a new desired state.

This requires on-going diligence and constant effort which soon gets tiresome and boring. The student usually gives up in frustration. The main reason for limited success is because of limiting beliefs. Old limiting beliefs must be removed. Trying to overpower them is not the best use of time and energy.

What's required for permanent change in your experience is a shift in focus from trying to overpower old beliefs with new ones, to a focus on identifying and simply dissolving the old beliefs that no longer serve you. These limiting beliefs may have been appropriate when you were a child, but as an adult they hinder you.

It's like planting a flower garden. If you don't first till the soil and pull out all the weeds before you plant, you'll end up with a field of weeds that has some flowers in it. An improvement, but not the desired result. Till the soil, remove the weeds, and now plant your seeds. In no time at all you'll have a marvelous garden of your favorite flowers.

Another way to look at the same concept would be like trying to hit the bull's eye on a target on the other side of a corn field. The corn stalks (limiting beliefs) resist and deflect the path of the arrow. Rather than try and brute force the arrow through the corn by pulling harder on the string, simply remove the corn stalks between you and the target. Now, with an accurate aim and normal pull, a bull's-eye is assured.

Develop Your Latent Paranormal Powers

People spend significant effort and money looking for ways to get what they want–happiness, money, love, jobs, only to give up in frustration. The secret is to focus on dissolving barriers – those barriers are the limiting beliefs that are generating your life's frustrations and fears.

We all have the ability to create our own environment, whether that environment be positive or negative. It all exists within the mind. We can actually change our own events in our lives by practicing the art of being positive. We have the power as co-creators with our higher consciousness.. We have that endowed power within, yet so few really understand how to use it properly.

The ability to think seems to set us apart from other creatures. And although we are concerned with living in the physical world, we are mental beings. The fact is we are thinking all the time. We plan, we brood, we get depressed or elated – all of it is thought. But the universe is mental too, and if we could control our thinking we would see magnificent results in the everyday world. Many systems have been developed over the ages to help us control our thoughts.

A great amount of dogma too has been kicked around in an attempt to make us into better people. Magick is one of the oldest and most general of these systems. Magick is the study and application of psychic forces. It uses mental training, concentration, and a system of symbols to program the mind. The purpose of magick is to alter the self and the environment according to the will.   We may theorize that the human mind and body broadcasts a kind of psychic energy or force, much like a radio station. Kirlian photography, temperature effects, cloud chamber tests, and other experiments tend to support this theory. Although the exact nature of this psychic force is subtle and unknown, it is undoubtedly the energy behind all psychic phenomena and magick.

The psychic force is too weak to be measured directly (at least so far as we know). Everyone has some psychic ability, but few recognize how easy it is to control and use these abilities. Magick encompasses many things -- science and art, philosophy and metaphysics, psychology and comparative religion. Magick is an adventure at the borderlands of the unknown. It can fit the pieces of the puzzle of life into a meaningful whole.

Magick is fun and interesting. Use magick to help raise consciousness without drugs. Gain new experiences. Fantasy can come alive through magick. Psychic phenomena can be controlled and be fun and helpful. Magick is beneficial. It can help you to have excellent health, and bring you good luck. With magick life runs smoothly; life is good. Also use magick for personality improvement, to control bad habits and to develop new motivations.

Magick is powerful. Never underestimate the tremendous power of magick. Use magick to alter events and to achieve your goals. Exert an influence over people and

Develop Your Latent Paranormal Powers

phenomena. But power for its own sake is self defeating. The power which magick can give you should not be your primary reason for studying it.

Your awareness of the physical world and of your place within it is mostly based upon the physical senses (hearing, sight, smell, touch, taste). These five senses continually send information to the mind, and it is up to the mind to select and interpret them. If you could not do so, your senses would overwhelm you and be meaningless.

Selection and interpretation of your sensory inputs is essentially an automatic, mostly subconscious function of the mind. The program or map which the subconscious follows as its reference point is called a 'model.' The model is a subconscious, mental photograph of how you believe the world looks (ie. worldview, mindset, egregore, or belief system).

It was built up from an early age by your religious and cultural background through interaction with family and others. It contains your experiences, attitudes, and habits. And whether you realize it or not, most of your behavior, thoughts, feelings, and habits are based upon and conditioned by that model; even personality. The model is one of the mind's master programs. Change in behavior generally requires a change in the model. These limitations built into our way of thinking cause our perceptions to be subjective. That is why Hindu philosophy looks upon the world as illusory (maya); the world itself (object) is not an illusion, however from our viewpoint through perception (subject) it is.

Thus we are all conditioned by experience. Except that our perceptions, hence our experiences, are first conditioned and limited by the model. Our perceptions and experiences tend to conform to what we expect. We tend to misinterpret or ignore things which do not match our preconceived notions about them. This is automatic.

The Magick of Psychic Powers

Though numerous religions, philosophies, and occult systems abound, they do not contradict one and other as much as it might appear. Rather, they describe the same (universal) reality taken from different perspectives. For there can be no ultimate truth in the physical world. We can only base our actions upon assumptions and agreements.

There is a separate reality within each of us which is often ignored unless we seek it. This inner self is in magick called the 'true will.' The true will is the center of consciousness and identity. It is the 'real you.' Everything else is an interface or link to it from the outer (illusory) world. Since that interface is based upon our model, it

Develop Your Latent Paranormal Powers

is conditioned and may sometimes produce false information.

"Do what thou wilt" (Crowley) is an principle of magick; for the true will expresses our exact desires. And what we truly want (down deep) we tend to automatically get. This isn't always in our best interests, since the true will can be conditioned (tricked) by the illusion; and then we might desire and obtain that which is not ultimately good for us. The task of the magician therefore is to awaken his awareness of the true will, to be free of conditioning, and thereby to transcend maya.

There is no great secret to changing behavior or habits. It is largely a matter of determination. It requires that you ignore the 'pull' of the model when you strive for changes within yourself. The model is, after all, a collection of 'habits,' some of which must be unlearned for permanent change to occur.

Emotions follow physical expression: smile and act happy and you will tend to feel and be happy. The same is also true for other emotions. Also, emotions can be purposely used (or programmed) to replace other emotions. Using this technique, a magician is somewhat like an actor in that he learns how to turn his emotions on and off at will.

Note that this is not faking it; the magician is probably more in touch with his true feelings than most people. And for these reasons we say that happiness is being happy.

Magick and paranormal abilities have always involves self-hypnosis. However, it may be more than that. For one thing, there are objective forces involved (or so it would seem). Deities, spirits, and cosmic force can have an independent existence. And the repetitive physical movement sometimes involved in ritual can itself generate PK force.

On the other hand, it could be argued that all of this is subjective to the magician. Or that the deities and spirits are nothing more than architypes or cosmic patterns which the magician energizes with his own vitality. Perhaps all magical effects could be produced through hypnosis alone. But the effects are certainly real.

Great complexity is not necessary in magick. Although basically magick is a medieval system of symbolism (in a modern context), any cosmological system will work from Cabala to Star Wars. We usually use the medieval one in magick because it is convenient and traditional, and because it seems to fit our thought processes well.

Traditional symbols have greater emotional effect on the magician than modern ones because of his familiarity with them. What really matters is that the model of the magician be understood and programmed, and thus that the model and the cosmological system do correspond.

The astral body (subconscious) is the intermediary for intuition, magical and psychic phenomena, and is the 'psychic link' to the physical world. J.H. Brennan says

Develop Your Latent Paranormal Powers

that the astral is the realm of visual imagination. It seems to be both a 'place' and a 'state of mind' at the same time. Most occult and magical phenomena originate in the invisible, non-sensate, non-physical realm (ie. without physical senses).

Each of the four worlds interacts with the other worlds. Psychic energy flows from the spiritual to mental to astral to physical. The physical world is a projection (manifestation, reflection, or shadow) of the higher worlds. Our center of consciousness is generally within these higher worlds.

The greater universe, known as the macrocosm, includes everything that exists. It corresponds with the microcosm, or tiny universe, ie. man – who is thought of as a miniature replica of the macrocosm (whole universe). This basic magical relationship is demonstrated in the Bible (Genesis 1.27), where God is the macrocosm; and in the writing of Trismegistus ("As above so below").

Since man is in the image of God (universe) it follows that God is in the image of man (in other words, man and the God/universe match each other). The magician, as a microcosm is thus connected with the macrocosm. There is an intimate relationship of energies between you and everything else. The universe is reflected within us and we are projected into the universe. This is an important theory behind magick and astrology.

Personal magick is that magick used to affect the self; often involving affirmation, self-suggestion, and self-hypnosis. Active magick is outer directed magick (as in PK) used to affect someone or thing, or to bring about an event. Passive magick is to be affected (as in ESP) by an outside non-physical cause. Everyone possesses some magical (and psychic) potential. Some are especially gifted. Usually people are better at one kind of magick (ie. active or passive) than they are at the other kind; only rarely does an individual excel at both. Training and practice will, of course, improve ability somewhat.

What we have been calling 'magick' is actually a continuous process. Since your subconscious never rests, your environment is continually being shifted into line with your model. This is true whether you study magick or not.

For most people, these effects are usually very subtle, and they are probably not aware of them. However, as you work with the occult, the flow of psychic energy and your awareness of it increases. Your true will is more likely to be strongly expressed. Your luck may be affected (either in a positive or a negative way). Remember, our lives tend to follow what we want down deep. That is why a positive outlook is so very beneficial to us.

The mind is always open to suggestion -- especially the subconscious. Most of the time we censor any suggestions according to the model; but one way to break through the censor is with repetition. An affirmation does this exactly. By suggestion, we mean any statement which is capable of affecting your model. Usually

Develop Your Latent Paranormal Powers

suggestion is in the form of a positive statement (such as the hypnotist's patter – "You are becoming sleepy"). An affirmation is the same kind of thing – a positive suggestion, which you repeat (affirm) to yourself aloud or silently (for example, "I remember my dreams").

If there is some quality you wish to change or develop within yourself, an affirmation is ideal. Repeat it several times every day at several different times throughout the day, especially when you go to bed. Affirmations are subtle and may require a few months to work. Use them for changes, not miracles.

Visualization is another important method we use to influence the subconscious. A good example of this is the simple banishing technique which follows. Banishing is used in magick to 'clear the air' of negative 'vibes' and interference.

Visualize a strong white light flowing out the top of your head, flowing down around you and covering you. At the same time imagine you are throwing away any 'problem' vibes. Maintain the visualization for a half a minute or longer. Good way to help you handle your emotions, and to control worry or anger.

You are now ready to take the next big step and learn to develop your latent paranormal powers. Now is the time to change your life for the better. With this book you will learn that there are amazing energies in the universe, and these energies also flow through you.

This book will change your life forever. You will see clearly for the first time that you do not have to be afraid – that you have complete control over your actions and ultimately your life. The universe is yours – it is a wonderful time to be alive.

So come along and allow my fellow practitioner and co-writer to instruct you in the various ways to expand your awareness and metaphysical knowledge. I am sure that you will be as impressed as I was with what Sir William Walker Atkinson has to say and teach you in the next section of this book titled: ***Practical Psychomancy***.

Set the foundation now. This will assure you a comfortable secure tomorrow.

Practical Psychomancy
and Crystal Gazing

LESSON I.
THE NATURE OF PSYCHOMANCY.

THE TERM "Psychomancy" (pronounced, "sy-ko-man-see"), is derived from two Greek words, the first "psycho," meaning "the soul; the mind; the understanding" (and generally used to indicate "psychic" or unusual powers of the soul or mind); the second word, "mancy" meaning "to divine; to foresee, or foreknow; to detect secret tbings,"—and in occult parlance, "to *sense*," or "to receive impressions by the Astral Senses." So the word, as we use it, may be said to mean "Psychic Sensing," and in this work will be so used. The word "Psychomancer" means "one practicing Psychomancy;" and the word "Psychomantic" means "relating to Psychomancy."

The word "Clairvoyance" is frequently used by people to designate some of the phases of Psychomancy, but strictly speaking this term is incorrect when used in this sense, the true occult meaning of the word "Clairvoyance," being "transcendental vision, or the perception of beings on another plane of existence—the seeing of disembodied souls, elementals, etc." And so, in this work, we shall consider the true phenomena of Clairvoyance, as distinct from that of Psychomancy.

In this work, we shall regard as the true phenomena of Psychomancy, all the various phenomena known as

Psychometry; Crystal Gazing; Perceiving Distant Scenes; a perception of Past Events, and Indication of Future Events; either in the full waking state; the state of reverie; or the state of dreams.

And, so this work will examine, consider, and explain, the various phases of phenomena above indicated—in short, the phenomena of *"sensing" objects by means of Astral Senses*, omitting the phenomena of Clairvoyance, or seeing disembodied souls, etc., which we regard as belonging to a different phase of the general subject, and which require special consideration and examination.

The majority of works upon these lines begin by an elaborate attempt to "prove" the reality of the phenomena in question. But we shall not fall into this error, for such we regard it. The time for the necessity of such proof is past. The records of the Societies for Psychical Research are full of proofs, and evidence, which are as full, complete and strong as ever required by any court to hang or clear a man. And the book shelves of the libraries are full of other books, giving like proof. And, for that matter, this work is not written to convince people of the truth of this phenomena—it is intended for those who have already convinced themselves of its reality, but who wish for specific information regarding its nature, manner of manifestation, etc. Where we quote instances of the manifestation of some form of Psychomantic phenomena, in this work, we do so simply to illustrate the characteristics of some particular form of the phenomena, and not as corroborative proof. With this explanation, we propose plunging right into the main subject itself.

There have been many attempted explanations of, and theories regarding the phenomena of Psychomancy, some of which are more or less plausible, while others are quite visionary, "wild," and fantastic. In this work, we shall pay no attention to those more or less ingenious "guesses" of the theorists, but shall, instead, give you plainly, clearly, and simply, the time-honored teachings of the advanced Occultists which teachings we believe to be the Truth, tested and tried by centuries of investigation, and experiment.

THE ASTRAL SENSES.

The Occult Teachings inform us that in addition to the Five Physical Senses possessed by man, viz: Seeing; Feeling; Hearing; Tasting; and Smelling; each of which has its appropriate sense organ, every individual is also possessed of Five Astral Senses, which form a part of what is known to Occultists as the Astral Body. These Astral Senses, which are the astral counterparts of the five physical senses, operate upon what Occulists call the Astral Plane, which is next above the Physical Plane, in the Sevenfold Scale of Planes. Just as do the Physical Senses operate upon the Physical Plane, so do the Astral Senses operate upon the Astral Plane.

By means of these Astral Senses, one may *sense* outside objects without the use of the physical senses usually employed. And it is through this sensing by these Astral Senses, that the phenomena of Psychomancy becomes possible.

By the employment of the Astral Sense of Seeing, the Psychomancer is able to perceive occurrences, scenes, etc., at a distance sometimes almost incredibly far; to see through solid objects; to see records of past occurrences in the Astral Ether; and to see Future Scenes thrown ahead in Time, like the shadows cast by material objects—"coming events cast their shadows before," you have heard. By the use of the Astral Sense of Hearing, he is able to sense sounds over immense distances and often after the passage of great periods of time, for the Astral vibrations continue for many years.

The Astral senses of Taste and Smell are seldom used, although there are abundant proofs of their existence. The Astral Sense of Feeling enables the Psychomancer to become aware of certain occurrences on the Astral Plane, and to perceive impressions, mental and otherwise, that are being manifested at a distance.

The Astral Sense of Feeling may be explained as being rather a sense of "Awareness," than of a mere "Feeling," inasmuch as the Psychomancer, through its channel, becomes "aware" of certain occurrences, other than by Astral Sight or Hearing, and yet which is not "Feeling" as the word is used on the Physical Plane. It may be well called "Sensing" for want of a better name, and manifests in a vague consciousness or "awareness." But still we must not overlook the fact that there are many instances of true "feeling," on the Astral Plane, for instances, cases where the Psychomancer actually "feels" the pain of another, which phenomena is commonly known as "sympathetic pains;" "taking on the condition," etc., etc., and which are well known to all investigators as belonging to the phenomena of the Astral Senses.

THE ASTRAL BODY.

But, to understand the Astral Senses, one must be made acquainted with the existence of that which Occultists know as "The Astral Body." There is no point in the Occult Teachings better established; longer held; or more thoroughly proven than that of the existence of the Astral Body. This teaching of the Ancient Occultists is being corroborated by the experiments, and investigations of the Psychic Researchers of the present day.

The Astral Body, belonging to every person, is an exact counterpart of the perfect physical body of the person. It is composed of fine ethereal matter, and is usually encased in the physical body. In ordinary cases, the detaching of the Astral Body from its physical counterpart is accomplished only with great difficulty, but in the case of dreams; great mental stress; and under certain conditions of occult development, the Astral Body may become detached and sent on long journeys, traveling at a rate of speed greater than that of light waves. On these journeys it is always connected with the physical body by a long filmy connecting link. If this link were to become broken, the person would die instantly, but this is an almost unheard

6

of occurrence in the ordinary planes of action. The Astral Body exists a long time after the death of the physical body, but it disintegrates in time. It sometimes hovers around the resting place of the physical corpse, and is mistaken for the "spirit" of the deceased person, although really it is merely a shell or finer outer coating of the soul. The Astral Body of a dying person is often projected to the presence of friends and loved ones a few moments before the physical death, the phenomenon arising from the strong desire of the dying person to see and be seen.

The Astral Body frequently travels from its physical counterpart, in Psychomantic phenomena, and visits scenes far distant, there sensing what is occurring. It also leaves the body during what are known as Psychomantic dreams; or under the influence of anaesthetics; or in some of the deeper phases of hypnosis; when it visits strange scenes and places, and often holds mental conversation with other Astral Bodies, or else with disembodied entities. The jumbled and distorted recollections of these dreams are occasioned by the brain not having received perfect impressions transmitted to it, by reason of lack of training, development, etc., the result being like a blurred or distorted photographic plate.

In order to intelligently grasp the underlying principles of the phenomena of Psychomancy, and its allied subjects, you must familiarize yourself with the truth concerning the Astral Senses, which we have just stated. Unless you understand and accept this truth and fact, you will not be able to grasp the principles underlying the phenomena in question, but will be lost in the quagmire of idle theories, and fantasic "explanation" hazarded by investigators of psychic phenomena who have not made themselves acquainted with the Occult Teachings which alone give the student an intelligent key to the mysteries of the Astral Plane.

THE THREE CLASSES.

The phenomena of Psychomancy, etc., may be grouped into three classes, each being produced by its own special class-cause. In either or all cases, the impressions are received by and through the Astral Senses, but there are three distinct ways in which, and by which, these impressions are received. These ways, which we shall now proceed to consider in detail, may be classified under the following terms:

(1) Sensing by the "quickening" of one's Astral Senses sufficient to perceive more clearly the etheric vibrations or currents; the auric emanations of persons and things; and similar phases of Psychomancy, but which does not include the power to sense occurrences happening in distant places; nor the power to sense the records of the past, or to receive indications of the future. (See Lesson III.)

(2) Sensing by means of the "Astral Tube," erected in the Ether by the operation of one's Will or Desire, and which acts as a Psychic "telescope," or "microscope," with "X Ray" features. (See Lesson IV.)

(3) Sensing by means of the actual projection of one's own Astral Body to the distant scene. (See Lesson VII.)

CLAIRAUDIENCE.

"Clairaudience" is a term sometimes used to indicate Astral Hearing. Some writers on this subject treat "Clairaudience" as a separate class of phenomena. But we fail to see the distinction they make. It, of course, employs a different Astral Sense from that generally employed, but both are Astral Senses functioning on the Astral Plane, just as the physical senses of Seeing and Hearing function on the Physical Plane. And, more important, both forms of Astral Sensing are subject to the same laws and rules. In other words, all that is said in the lessons of this book on the subject of Psychomantic Vision holds equally true of Clairaudience.

Thus, there may be Simple *Clairaudience*; Space *Clairaudience*; Past Time *Clairaudience*; Future Time *Clairaudience*, etc.; also *Clairaudient* Psychometry; *Clairaudience* through Crystal Gazing, etc. Psychomantic Vision is the employment of the Astral *Sight*, while Clairaudience is the similar employment of the Astral *Hearing*.

In many cases of Psychomantic Vision there Is an accompaniment of Clairaudience; while in others it may be missing. Likewise, Psychomantic Vision usually accompanied Clairaudience, although sometimes one may be able to *hear* astrally, although not seeing.

You will notice that in many of the instances of Psychomantic Vision related in this book, there is a mention of the person *hearing* words or sounds, while seeing the vision—this, of course, is Clairaudience.

Lesson II.

How to Develop Yourself.

PASSING TO the actual practice, we desire to inform our students that the faculty of Psychomancy lies dormant in every person—that is the Astral Senses are present in everyone, and the possibility of their being awakened into activity is always present. The different degrees of power observable in different persons depend chiefly upon the degree of development, or unfoldment, rather than upon the comparative strength of the faculties. In some persons, of certain temperaments, the Astral Senses are very near the manifesting point at all times. Flashes of what are considered to be "intuition," premonitions, etc., are really manifestations of Psychomancy in some phase. In the case of other persons, on the other hand, the Astral Senses are almost atrophied, so merged in materialistic thought and life are these people. The element of Faith also plays an important point in this phenomena, as it does in all Occult phenomena, for that matter. That is to say, that one's *belief* tends to open up the latent powers and faculty in man, while a corresponding *disbelief* tends to prevent the unfoldment or manifestation. There is a very good psychological reason for this as all students of the subject well know. Belief and Disbelief are two potent psychological factors on all planes of action.

Occultists know, and teach, that the Astral Senses and faculties of the human race will unfold as the race progresses, at which time that which we now call Psychomantic Power will be a common possession of all persons, just as the use of the Physical Senses are to the race at the present time. In the meantime, there are persons who, not waiting for the evolution of the race, are beginning to manifest this power in a greater or lesser degree, depending much upon favorable circumstances, etc. There are many more persons in this stage of development than is generally realized. In fact many persons manifesting Psychomantic power, occasionally, are apt to pass by the phenomena as "imagination," and "foolishness," refusing to recognize its reality. Then, again, many persons manifest the power during sleeping hours, and dismiss the matter as "merely a dream," etc.

Regarding this matter of the dawning of Psychomancy, a well-known authority writes as follows: "Students often ask how this psychic faculty will first be manifested in themselves—how they may know when they have reached the stage at which its first faint foreshadowings are beginning to be visible. Cases differ so widely that it is impossible to give to this question an answer that will be universally applicable. Some people begin by a plunge, as it were, and under some unusual stimulus become able just for once to see some striking vision; and very often in such a case, because the experience does not repeat itself, the seer comes in time to believe that on that occasion he must have been the victim of hallucination. Others begin by becoming intermittently conscious of the brilliant colors and vibrations of the human aura; others find themselves with increasing frequency seeing and hearing something to which those around them are blind and deaf; others again see faces, landscapes, or colored clouds floating before their eyes in the dark, before they sink to rest; while perhaps the commonest experience of all is that of those who begin to recollect with greater and greater clearness what they have seen and heard on other planes during sleep."

Very many persons possess respectable degrees of Simple Psychomancy, varying from vague impressions to the full manifestation of the faculty, as described in these lessons. Such a person has "intuitions"; "notions"; "presentiments," and the faculty of getting ideas regarding other persons and things, other than by the usual mental processes. Others manifest certain degrees of Psychometric powers, which develop rapidly by practice. Others find themselves possessing certain degrees of power of "scrying" through Crystals, which power, also, may be developed by practice. The phases of Time Psychomancy, Past and Future; and that of Space Psychomancy, in its higher degrees, are far more rare, and few persons possess them, and still fewer persist in the practice until they develop it, they lacking the patience, persistence, and application necessary.

While it is very difficult to lay down a set method of instruction in the Development of Psychomantic Power, owing to reasons already given, and because of the varying temperaments, etc., of students, yet there is possible a plan of giving general information, which if followed will put the student upon the right path toward future development. And this plan we shall now proceed to give the students of this little book.

DEVELOPMENT METHODS.

Concentration. In the first place, the student should cultivate the faculty of Concentration, that is the power to hold the attention upon an object for some time. Very few persons possess this power, although they may think they do. The best way to develop Concentration is to practice on some familiar and common object, such as a pencil, book, ornament, etc. Take up the object and study it in detail, forcing the mind to examine and consider it in every part, until every detail of the object has been observed and noted. Then lay the object aside, and a few hours after pick it up again and repeat the process, and you will be surprised to see how many points you have missed on the first trial. Repeat this until you feel that you have exhausted your object. The next day take up another object, and repeat the process. A drill of this kind will not only greatly develop the powers of Perception, but will also strengthen your powers of Concentration in a manner which will be of great value to you in Occult Development.

Visualizing. The second point of development for the student, is the development of the faculty of Visualization. In order to Visualize you must cultivate the faculty of forming Mental Pictures of distant scenes, places, people, etc., until you can summon them before you at will, when you place yourself in the proper mental condition. Another plan is to place yourself in a comfortable position, and then make a mental journey to some place that you have previously visited. Prepare for the journey, and then mentally see yourself starting on your trip; then seeing all the intermediate places and points; then arriving at your destination and visiting the points of interest, etc.; and then returning home. Then, later try to visit places that you have never seen, in the same way. This is not Clairvoyance, but is a training of the mental faculties for the exercise of the real power.

Psychometry. After you have developed yourself along the lines of Concentration, and Visualization as above stated, you may begin to practice Psychometry, as follows: Take a lock of hair; or handkerchief; or ribbon; or ring; belonging to some other person, and then press it against your forehead, lightly, closing your eyes, and assuming a receptive and passive mental state. Then desire calmly that you Psychometrize the past history of the object. Do not be in too much of a hurry, but await calmly the impressions. After a while you will begin to receive impressions concerning the person owning the object pressed against your forehead. You will form a mental picture of the person, and will soon begin to receive impressions about his characteristics, etc. You may practice with a number of objects, at different times, and will gradually develop the Psychometric power by such practice and experiments. Remember that you are developing what is practically a new sense and must have perseverance and patience in educating and unfolding it.

Another form of Psychometric development is that of tracing the past history, surroundings, etc., of metals, minerals, etc. The process is identical to that just described. The mineral is pressed against the forehead, and with closed eyes the person awaits the Psychometric impression. Some who have highly developed the faculty have been able to describe the veins of mineral, metal, etc., and to give much valuable information regarding same, all arising from the psychic clue afforded by a sample of the rock. mineral, metal, etc. There are other cases of record, in which underground streams of water have been discovered by Psychometrists, by means of the clue given by a bit of earth, stone, etc., from the surface. In this, as in the other phase mentioned, *practice, practice, practice*, is the summing up of the instruction regarding development.

Crystal Gazing. We consider the use of the Crystal, Glass Ball, or other forms of what the ancients called "The Magic Mirror," to be the best plan of developing Psychomantic Power. As we have already explained, this method serves to focus the concentrated desire, will, and thought of the person, and thereby becomes the starting point for the Astral Tube, of which we have frequently spoken in this work. The student becoming proficient in this class of phenomena, passes by easy, gradual and natural stages to the higher and more complex phases of the subject. The "Magic Mirror" (of which the Crystal is but a form) was used by the ancient Occultists in developing the powers of their students, and in all countries, and in all ages, it has played a similar part in the process of developing psychic powers, and serving as a focal point for the erection and operation of the Astral Tube, Psychomancy and other forms of occult and psychic phenomena.

At this point, we wish to tell you that there is no special virtue or magical properties or qualities in the Crystal itself—it is merely an instrument for Astral Vision, just as the telescope, microscope and other optical instruments are instruments employed in the phenomena of physical vision. It is true that the atomic and molecular characteristics of glass, crystal, etc., tend to produce the best results, but, after all, water, ink, etc., have been, and may be similarly used. No, there is no special "magic" in the crystal itself, so do not allow yourself to fall into any superstition regarding its use.

Various teachers use different forms of the Crystal, or substitutes for it. Some of the teachers whose patrons are among the wealthier classes of the community, insist upon their pupils possessing globes of pure crystal, insisting that the latter alone gives the best results. But others who have pupils among people with shorter purses, have found that their pupils obtained just as good results by the use of a ball of plain glass, which is inexpensive. Others have advocated the use of watch crystals laid over a piece of black cloth, preferably velvet. Others have used polished steel objects, or pieces of polished metal of various kinds, a new silver coin, for instance. Others still, have used a large drop of ink poured into a small dish, etc. Others have had cups painted black on their inner surface, into which they poured water, and claimed to have obtained the finest results. All the old talk about magic ceremonies and incantations being necessary in manufacturing the Magic Mirror, is pure nonsense, which has grown around the scientific facts of the case, as is so often the case. Do not be deceived by any such tomfoolery. A number of persons prefer to gaze into the bright substance of a precious stone. So you see, when we use the term "Crystal," we mean that the student may make his choice of any, or several, of the above-mentioned objects, or that he may even substitute some other object of his own choosing, possessing the requisite power of reflection.

There are but very few directions to be given in the use of the Crystal. Read what we have to say at the conclusion of our lesson on "Crystal Gazing" in this book, (Lesson VI). The principal point insisted upon by nearly all the teachers, is that of placing the back of the gazer to the light, instead of having him face the light.

The simple general direction is that the gazer should practice by himself, at first, in a quiet room, sitting with his back toward the light, with the Crystal placed before him on a table, on a piece of black cloth, or other dark material, and then gaze calmly at the Crystal. Do not be afraid of winking, and do not strain or tire the eyes. Some prefer making funnels of their hands, and gazing through them just as if they were opera-glasses, and we think this plan a very good one, for it serves to shut out distracting light, and sights. If you fail to see anything at the first trial, do not be discouraged, but persevere. A number of trials are necessary in some cases, while in others wonderful results have been obtained at the first experiment.

An English authority recommends that beginners failing to get direct results, then try to "visualize" something that they have already seen—something familiar, such as a chair, a ring, a face, etc., and then turning to the Crystal endeavor to reproduce there. It is claimed that this practice will often gradually lead to actual "seeing" in the Crystal.

The first signs of the actual "seeing" in the Crystal, comes in the form of a "cloudiness," or "milky-mist" in the crystal, which slowly resolves itself into a form, or scene, which appears gradually like the precipitation of a photograph upon a sensitive plate in the developing room. In some cases, the "misty" cloud deepens into a black one, from which the pictures appear.

General Advice. In this work we give you a comprehensive, although condensed, account of the various phases of the phenomena of Psychomancy, together with a number of instances of typical manifestations. By reading the following lessons, after having read the present one, the student will be able to gather much practical instruction on the subject of the manifestation of the power. He will be able to understand the nature and general workings of the phenomena, so that, when he undertakes the work of developing the power within himself, he will recognize the indication of his increasing power and unfolding faculties, which otherwise would "be Greek" to him. In order to get the very best results of instruction in this line, the student would of course do well to secure some competent instructor who could give him personal lessons. But, the person who has the patience and perseverance to "work the thing out for himself," as many before him have done, will obtain results none the less valuable because they were worked for without assistance.

We feel that we have given the students of this little work, such an idea of the general subject, and its fundamental laws, together with such general instruction in the methods of developing and manifesting the power that it will be one's own fault if he fails to get at least a fair degree of success from his undertaking self-development along these lines. There is no royal road to occult or psychic power—no "magic word" which when once pronounced will prove an "open Sesame" to the Doors of Psychomancy. And we would warn the student against persons who undertake to impart the "Secret" upon the payment of a goodly sum of money. There is no "Secret" to be so imparted—it is all a matter, first of general understanding, and then practice and work. To some it comes easier than to others, but even to such, the higher degrees mean work and practice. We trust that we have given you food for thought and material for practice. The rest depends upon yourself.

LESSON III.
SIMPLE PSYCHOMANCY.

THE PHENOMENA of Psychomancy may be divided into three general classes, depending upon the nature of the "seeing," as follows:

I. Simple Psychomancy, by which is meant the power of "sensing" by means of the Astral Senses in the degree of a mere "quickening" of the Astral Senses sufficiently to enable one to "sense" more clearly any etheric vibrations or currents; the auric emanations of persons and things; and similar phases of Psychomantic phenomena; but which does not include the power to sense actual occurrences happening in distant places; nor the power to sense the records of the past, or to receive indications of the future.

II. Space Psychomancy, by which is meant the power to sense *distant* scenes, persons, or objects.

III. Time Psychomancy, by which is meant the power to sense objects, events, persons, etc., in the records of the past; and also the power to sense the indications of the future—the "shadows of coming events."

Simple Psychomancy is very much more common than is generally supposed. Very many people are quite sensitive to "impressions" coming to them in this way, which while akin to the impressions of Telepathy, nevertheless belong to the higher grade of Psychic Phenomena known as Psychomancy. It may be well to state here the difference between ordinary Telepathic impressions, and those of Simple Psychomancy. Many students are perplexed by the similarity between the two mentioned classes of phenomena, and we think it advisable to set them straight regarding the matter, at this point.

As we have stated in our previous work in this series, (entitled "Practical Mind Reading") Telepathy is occasioned by the passage of Thought Waves or Currents, passing from one brain to another, just as pass the waves of Heat, Light, Electricity, etc. In Telepathy the brain of the Transmitter sends forth the vibration, waves, or currents, and the brain of the Receiver registers the same, receiving them by means of the Pineal Gland which acts in a manner closer resembling that of the receiving instrument in Wireless Telegraphy. In Telepathy there is merely the sending and receiving of thought vibrations, *over the physical organs.*

But in Simple Psychomancy, the person may, and does, receive the thought vibrations emanating from the mind of another, but not over the physical channels, as in Telepathy, *but by means of the Astral Senses.* In this lies the difference.

Now, it follows that the Astral Senses being far more keen and acute than the Physical Senses, the former will register vibrations and impressions far more readily than the latter, and will often register impressions that the Physical Senses (even the Pineal Gland organ) take no account of. In this way the person in whom the Astral Senses are even partially developed will receive impressions of the thoughts of others that even the most acute Mind Reader will fail to notice; as well as words actually spoken by the other person; and ideas forming in the mind of the other person not yet expressed in active thought-waves.

But, it should be added, the development of Telepathic powers very frequently grow into a development of Psychomantic powers, and so the former is one of the easiest paths to the latter, and may be used in developing Clairvoyant power, and in unfolding the Astral Senses. In this way the person possessing even a moderate degree of Psychomantic power often "feels" the thoughts, ideas, emotions, and other mental states of the people around him, and knows without any words being used just what the others are thinking and feeling. This is often perceived by merely the increased power to receive and register the Thought-vibrations, but in some cases the ability to sense the "Aura" of the other persons heighten the impression.

THE AURA.

The majority of our readers are familiar with the fact that all persons, and objects, are surrounded by an emanation called an "Aura," or egg-shaped psychic emanation extending several feet around them. This aura is charged with the thought-vibrations of the persons, and is really the "atmosphere" that we feel surrounding people and by which we feel attracted or repelled as the case may be. The trained and developed Psychomancer is able to see the colors by which the various emotions, thoughts, etc., are indicated, but even when that degree of power is lacking, he may "feel" the general character of the various component parts of the person's aura.

While it is not our intention to go deeply into this matter of Auric Colors, in this work, still we think it well to indicate the same here, by quoting from a well-known authority on the subject, who says: "As he looks at a person he will see him surrounded by the luminous mist of the astral aura, flashing with all sorts of brilliant colors, and constantly changing in hue and brilliancy with every variation of the person's thoughts and feelings. He will see this aura flooded with the beautiful rose-color of pure affection; the rich blue of devotional feeling; the hard dull brown of selfishness; the deep scarlet of anger; the horrible lurid red of sensuality; the livid grey of fear; the black clouds of hatred and malice; or any of the other hundredfold indications so easily to be read in it by a practiced eye; and thus it will be impossible for any persons to conceal from him the real state of their feelings on any subject."

But only a comparatively few are able to distinctly *see* these Auric Colors, by reason of their lack of development along these special lines. But a great number of people are able to *feel* the subtle vibrations which give rise to these colors. Just as there are well authenticated cases of blind men and women being able to distinguish by the sense of feeling (in touch) the various colors which their blind eyes fail to see, so are thousands of people able to *feel* the auric shades which their imperfectly developed clairvoyant vision fails to perceive. In this connection it is interesting to note that science informs us that the sense of Feeling was the first developed of any of the physical senses; in fact all the other senses are developments of, and extensions of, the original sense of Feeling. And there is a close correspondence between this phenomena of the Physical Senses, and that of the Astral Senses.

But there are other, and perhaps more wonderful, features of Simple Psychomancy. It is a well established scientific fact that nearly, if not indeed all, objects are constantly emanating streams of Radiant Energy, or Streams of Electrons as they are called by some. The delicate instruments of science are able to detect and register some of the coarser vibrations of this energy, but the more delicate ones have so far escaped them. But the Astral Senses of the developed Psychomancer register and record many of the finer vibrations, and in this way many so-called "miracles" of occultism are explained. Let us examine this phenomena at this point.

It becomes apparent to any student of the subject, early in his investigations, that the Psychomancer is able to "see" things hidden by other objects, and often surrounded by the densest matter. In other words he is able to *see through solid objects*— to see "through a brick wall" to use the familiar phrase. Now this may seem almost incredible to one at the first mention of the subject. But when the skeptic's attention is called to the fact that the "X Rays" and similar forms of energy recently discovered by science, readily pierce through solid objects, and may be actually "seen" by the eye (aided by the proper instruments), or recorded on a photographic plate—then the impossible feat of "seeing through a brick wall" becomes a very simple, understandable matter, indeed. And in an almost identical manner the Psychomancer *sees through solid objects—* and *the most solid material becomes transparent to his Astral Sight.*

The fine streams or waves of energy constantly being emanated by all objects, which are invisible to the naked physical eye, are registered and recorded by the Astral Sense of Sight. The Psychomancer even by means of the comparatively elementary power of Simple Psychomancy is able to see what is going on in an adjoining room, or other nearby place; to read the contents of a sealed letter; to describe the contents of a locked, steel book; or to read a chosen passage in a closed book.

To the developed and trained Psychomancer, when he concentrates his power, the solid ground over which he is walking, becomes transparent, and he is enabled to see down into its depths to a considerable distance. In this way he may see living underground creatures at work, and play; and to discover veins of mineral, coal, etc., or underground streams of water. In these cases the Clairvoyant *does not travel* in the Astral, but merely receives and perceives the subtle vibrations or streams of fine energy constantly being emanated by the objects. Some Clairvoyants have developed certain other less common faculties of Astral Sight, which give the "telescopic" and "microscopic" vision in these "cases, in addition to the main faculty of "seeing" things through solid coverings.

The question will naturally arise in the mind of the student, whether there is any limit to the depths open to the Astral Sight of the Psychomancer (in this phase of the phenomena), as for instance when he is looking into the solid earth. It may be urged that as objects at immense distances underground emanate rays just as truly as do objects nearer the surface, then there should be no difference in the power of vision. Answering this question we would say that the same objection and obstacle arises in this case, as in the corresponding physical phenomena, such as the X Rays. While a far distant object emits rays just as well as a nearby one, still there is a loss of energy according to distance, and the Astral Sense, like the Physical Sense, fails to clearly register after a certain distance is attained. This distance varies in the case of different persons using their Astral Vision, just as it does in the case of the different degrees of eyesight possessed by various persons. And then again, it must not be supposed that the earth becomes as clear as glass to the Astral Vision. On the contrary it presents a similar appearance to that obtained when one is seeing objects through water or mist, with the physical eye. One can see quite a way through water or mist with the physical eye, but after a certain distance the impressions grow dim, and finally fade from view. Of course in the case of the erecting of the Astral Tube better results may be obtained, but this phenomena belongs to the class of Space Psychomancy.

There is another power open to the Psychomancer along the lines of Simple Psychomancy. We refer to the phenomena of "seeing into" the physical bodies of other people; examining the internal organs; diagnosing diseases, etc. Of course, in this case, before the Clairvoyant is able to correctly diagnose a disease he must be acquainted with the nature of the organs, and their appearance in their normal state, etc., so that he will recognize a diseased condition when he sees it. One must needs have an acquaintance with Anatomy and Physiology, as well as possessing trained Psychomantic powers for this work.

LESSON IV.

THE ASTRAL TUBE.

THE TERM *"The Astral Tube,"* is frequently met with in the writings of Occultists, but you will find very little more than a mention of it in many of such works, the proverbial caution of the older writers having acted in the direction of preventing their entering into a fuller description or explanation, for fear of the information falling into improper hands. This will be more readily understood, when we tell you that the Astral Tube is, and may be, used for classes of phenomena other than that of Psychomancy, notably that of Mental Influencing, "treating," etc., which however forms no part of the present work, but which will be discussed in a future volume of the series to be called "Mental Influence, etc."

The Astral Plane is composed of an ethereal form of matter, very much rarer and finer than the matter of the Physical Plane—but matter, nevertheless, and subject to fixed laws and conditions. And, just as it is possible to establish "lines of force" in the physical matter, so may corresponding "lines of force" be established in Astral matter. And this Astral Tube is really such a "line of force." In other words, it is possible to set up and establish a "line of force" on the Astral Plane, that will serve as a ready conductor of Astral vibrations, currents, etc.,

25

and which affords a highly efficient channel of communication between objects far removed from each other in space. And this channel is actually created and used in a variety of forms of Occult phenomena.

POLARIZATION.

You have heard of "Polarity," and "Polarization" in connection with electrical phenomena. "Polarity" is defined by Webster as: "That quality or condition of a body by virtue of which it exhibits opposite or contrasted properties or powers, in opposite or contrasted parts or directions; or, a condition giving rise to a contrast of properties corresponding to a contrast of positions." And, "Polarization" is defined by the same authority as: "Act of polarizing; state of having polarity." Well, then, the process of erecting the Astral Tube is practically that of the "polarization" of the particles of Astral matter by an effort of the human Will, set in motion by means of a strong Desire or Determination, under certain conditions.

When the human Will is directed toward a distant person or object, under the proper psychic conditions, it tends to "polarize" a path or channel through the Astral atmosphere toward the desired point, which channel becomes at once an easy course of psychic communication for the transmission or receiving of psychic impressions or expressions, as the case may be. And, in the case of Psychomancy, and kindred phenomena, the Astral Senses of the person (even though his Astral Body be still within its physical counterpart) are able to readily "sense" the impressions being manifested at a far distant point in space.

The above mentioned channel of communication—the Astral Tube—has not of course the advantages of actual travel in the Astral Body, and is besides affected by certain Astral happenings, such as the breaking up of the tube, or an impairment of its efficiency, by reason of some stronger astral current or channel, etc., for instance. When one considers the currents and cross-currents constantly in operation on the

Astral Plane, it will be seen how likely the above mentioned interference is to happen.

Through the Astral Tube the Astral Senses actually "sense" the sights, and often the sounds, being manifested at a distance, just as one may see distant sights through a telescope, or hear distant sounds through a telephone, for instance. It also may be used as a microscope, as we shall see as we proceed. The student's attention is especially directed toward the fact that in this form of phenomena, the Psychomancer remains within his physical body, and does not travel in the Astral at all. He sees the distant scenes, just as a man sees them through a telescope. His consciousness remains within his physical body.

A well known writer on this subject has truly said: "...the limitations resemble those of a man using a telescope on the physical plane. The experimenter, for example, has a particular field of view which cannot be enlarged or altered: he is looking at his scene from a certain direction, and he cannot suddenly turn it all around and see how it looks from the other side. If he has sufficient psychic energy to spare, he may drop altogether the telescope that he is using, and manufacture an entirely new one for himself which will approach his objective somewhat differently; but this is not a course at all likely to be adopted in practice. But, it may be said, the mere fact that he is using Astral Sight ought to enable him to see it from all sides at once. And so it would, if he were using that sight in the normal way upon an object which was fairly near him—within his astral reach as it were; but at a distance of hundreds or thousands of miles the case is very different. Astral sight gives us the advantage of an additional dimension, but there is still such a thing as position in that dimension, and it is naturally a potent factor in limiting the use of the powers of its plane. ... Astral sight, when it is cramped by being directed along what is practically a tube, is limited very much as physical sight would be under similar circumstances, though if possessed in perfection it will continue to show, even at that distance, the auras, and therefore all the emotions and most of the thoughts of the people under observation."

The Astral Tube, in connection with Psychomancy, is used in a variety of forms. It is often used unconsciously, and springs into existence spontaneously, under the power of some strong emotion, desire or will. It is also observed in some cases of hypnotic phenomena, in which the hypnotist uses his will to cause his subject to form an Astral Tube, and then report his impressions. It is also used by the trained Psychomancer, without the use of any "starting point," or "focal centre," simply by the exercise of his trained, developed and concentrated will. But its most familiar and common use is in connection with some object serving as a "starting point," or "focal centre."

The "starting point" or "focal centre," above mentioned, is generally either what is known as "the associated object" in the class of phenomena commonly known as "Psychometry," or else a glass or crystal-ball, or similar polished reflecting surface, in what is known as "Crystal Gazing." In the two next succeeding lessons, we shall consider these two forms of phenomena, respectively.

LESSON V.

PSYCHOMETRY.

THE PHENOMENA commonly known as "Psychometry," is but one phase of Psychomancy—or it even may be said to be but a *method employed* to bring into action the Astral Senses. The Psychometrist merely *gets into rapport* with the distant scene; or period of time; or person; or object; by using some bit of physical material associated with that scene; time; person; objects; etc., into order to "open up communications" along the usual lines of Psychomancy. This has been compared to the use of objects associated with a thing in the case of memory. We all know how the sight of some object will recall at once memories of thinll long since forgotten, to all appearances, but which memories have been merely stored away in the great storehouse of the mind, to be recalled readily when the "association" is furnished. What "association" is in the case of Memory, so is the material object presented as the "associated object" in Psychometry.

The Occult Teachings inform us that *there is a psychic connection ever existing between things once associated*, and that when we throw ourselves into the psychic current surrounding an object we may readily follow the current back until we reach the associated object for which we are seeking on the Astral

Plane. In the Akashic Records (See Lesson IX) all memories are registered and recorded, and if we have a good starting point we may travel back until we find that which we desire. In the same way the "associated object" furnishes us with a ready means of starting our Astral Tube into being and use. This is the secret of the use of the lock of hair; the bit of clothing; the piece of metal or mineral, etc., used by Psychometrists.

A well known authority on the subject has said concerning Psychometry: "It may be asked how it is possible, amid the bewildering confusion of these records of the past, to find any particular picture when it is wanted? As a matter of fact, the untrained psychic usually cannot do so without some special link to put him in rapport with the subject required. Psychometry is an instance in point, and it is quite probable that our ordinary memory is really only another presentment of the same idea. It seems as though there were a sort of magnetic attachment or affinity between any particle of matter and the record which contains its history—an affinity which enables it to act as a kind of conductor between that record and the faculties of anyone who can read it. For instance, I once brought from Stonehenge a tiny fragment of stone, not larger than a pin's head, and on putting this into an envelope and handing it to a psychometrist who had no idea what it was, she at once began to describe the wonderful ruin from which it came, and the desolate country surrounding it, and then went on to picture vividly what were evidently scenes from its early history, showing that the infinitesimal fragment had been sufficient to put her into communication with the records connected with the spot from which it came. The scenes through which we pass in the course of our life seem to act in the same manner upon the cells of our brain as did the history of Stonehenge upon that particle of stone; they establish a connection with those cells by means of which our mind is put in rapport with that particular portion of the records, and so we 'remember' what we have seen."

PSYCHOMETRY.
THE FIVE METHODS.

The method of Psychometry may be employed in a number of ways, among which are the following, all of which are subject to many variations and combinations:

1. Locating a person by means of a lock of hair, article of clothing, handkerchief, ribbon, piece of jewelry, bit of writing, etc. In this manner not only may a good Psychometrist locate the person, but will also be able to give an idea of his characteristics, habits, health, etc.

2. Describing a person's characteristics, past life, future, etc., by means of the rapport condition made possible by the person's presence.

3. Describing a present distant scene by means of a bit of mineral, plant, or similar object once located at the place.

4. Describing the surrounding underground characteristics by means of a bit of mineral, etc.

5. Getting into touch with the past history of an object, or its surroundings, by means of the object itself. For instance, a bullet from the battle-field may give the history of the battle; a bit of ancient pottery, the characteristics and habits of the people who made or used it, as well as the appearance of the land in which they dwell, etc.

In all of these phases, with their variations and combination, the student will see the operation of the phenomena under the various heads as classified by us in this work. Each occurrence or manifestation will be found to fit into the class of Simple Psychomancy; Space Psychomancy; Past Time Psychomancy; or Future Time Psychomancy.

(See Lesson II, for suggestions regarding development of Psychometric power.)

LESSON VI.

CRYSTAL GAZING.

THERE HAS been a great revival of interest in the subject of "Crystal Gazing," particularly in England, of late years, and many interesting accounts have appeared in the papers and magazines regarding the results of the experiments. But the majority of the writers on the subject persist in treating it as a thing separate and apart from other forms of Psychomancy— in fact, many of them ignore Psychomancy altogether and are apparently under the impression that there is no connection between it and their favorite subject of Crystal Gazing. This attitude is somewhat amusing to persons who have made a careful study of Psychic Phenomena and who know that Crystal Gazing is not a distinct phenomenon, but is merely a method of bringing into action the Psychomantic faculties.

In many respects the Crystal acts in a manner akin to that of the "associated object" in Psychometry, but there is one point of distinction which should not be overlooked by the student. The "associated object" gives to the Psychometrist a *starting point for the Astral Tube*, and also serves to "point the Astral Telescope" (if one may use the term) in the right direction, by reason of its affinity with the distant scene, etc. But the Crystal does not so act, for it is not closely allied to, or in sympathy with other things, when used in the ordinary manner. Instead of being the "eye-lens of the telescope," it is really a "Magic Mirror" which is turned first this way and that, and which reflects whatever comes within its field, just as does any other mirror. The trained and developed Psychomancer, however, may direct his Mirror to any desired point, and may hold it there by means of a concentrated Will.

The favor with which Crystal Gazing meets with at the hands of beginners is due to the fact that it is the easiest method known by which the Astral Vision may be awakened. With the majority of people, the power may be awakened only by the aid of some physical object which may act as a starting-point for the Astral Tube, or as one writer has expressed it, "a convenient focus for the Will-power." A number of objects may be so employed, but the Crystal or Glass Ball is the best for the purpose because of certain atomic and molecular arrangements which tend to promote the manifestation of the psychic power and faculties.

Crystal Gazing, as a method for inducing Psychomantic vision, has been quite common among all peoples, in all times. Not only the Crystal but many other objects are . similarly used. In Australia the native priests use water and shining objects, or in some cases, flame. In New Zealand some of the natives use a drop of blood. The Fijians fill a hole with water, and gaze into it. Some South American tribes use the polished surface of a black stone. The American Indians used water and shining bits of flint or quartz. And so the story goes. As Lang states it, people "stare into a crystal ball; a cup; a mirror; a blot of ink (Egypt and India); a drop of blood (the Maoris of New Zealand); a bowl of water (American Indians); a pond (Roman and African); water in a glass bowl (Fez); or almost any polished surface, etc."

We quote a typical case of Crystal Gazing, related by Mr. Andrew Lang. He says: "I had given a glass ball to a young lady, Miss Baillie, who had scarcely any success with it. She lent it to Miss Leslie, who saw a large, square, old-fashioned red sofa covered with muslin (which she afterward found in the next country-house she visited). Miss Baillie's brother, a young athlete, laughed at these experiments, took the ball into his study, and came back looking 'gey gash.' He admitted that he had seen a vision—somebody he knew, under a lamp. He said he would discover during the week whether he saw right or not. This was at 5.30 on a Sunday afternoon. On Tuesday, Mr. Baillie was at a dance in a town forty miles from his home, and met a Miss Preston. 'On Sunday,' he said, 'about half-past five, you were sitting under a standard lamp, in a dress I never saw you wear, a blue blouse with lace over the shoulders, pouring out tea for a man in blue serge, whose back was towards me, so that I only saw the tip of his mustache! 'Why, the blinds must have been up,' said Miss Preston. 'I was at Dulby,' said Mr. Baillie, and he undeniably was."

Stead relates the following experience with the Crystal: "Miss X. upon looking into the crystal on two occasions as a test, to see if she could see men when she was several miles off, saw not me, but a different friend of mine on each occasion. She had never seen either of my friends before, but imediately identified them both on seeing them afterward at my office. On one of the evenings on which we experimented in the vain attempts to photograph a Double, I dined with Madam C. and her friend at a neighboring restaurant. As she glanced at the water bottle, Madam C. saw a picture beginning to form, and, looking at it from curiosity, described with considerable detail an elderly gentleman whom she had never seen before. and whom I did not in the least recognize from her description at the moment. Three hours afterwards, when the seance was over, Madam C. entered the room and recognized Mr. Elliott, of Messrs. Elliott & Fry, as the gentleman whom she had seen and described in the water bottle at the restaurant. On another occasion the picture was less agreeable: it was an old man lying dead in bed with some one weeping at his feet; but who it was, or what it related to, no one knew."

As a matter of general interest, we also quote Mr. Stead's remarks on crystal gazing, which agree with our own views and experience. He says: "There are some people who cannot look into an ordinary globular bottle without seeing pictures form themselves, without any effort or will on their part, in the crystal globe. Crystal gazing seems to be the least dangerous and most simple of all forms of experimenting. You simply look into a crystal globe the size of a five-shilling piece, or a water bottle which is full of clear water, and which is placed so that too much light does not fall upon it, and then simply look at it. You make no incantations, and engage in no mumbo-jumbo business; you simply look at it for two or three minutes, taking care not to tire yourself, winking as much as you please, but fixing your thought upon whatever you wish to see. Then, if you have the faculty, the glass will cloud over with a milky mist, and in the centre the image is gradually precipitated in just the same way as a photograph forms on the sensitive plate."

(See Lesson II, for further particulars on Crystal Gazing, and suggestions for the successful development of the power.)

Lesson VII.

Astral Projection.

I N OUR last three lessons we considered that class of Psychomancy arising from the erection and employment of the "Astral Tube." In the present lesson we pass to a consideration of the third class of phenomena, namely, that occasioned by the actual projection of one's Astral Body to distant points.

In this class of phenomena the consciousness of the person does not remain within the physical organism, but is actually projected along with the Astral Body to the point being psychically viewed or examined. This form of Psychomancy is, of course, a higher degree of manifestation than the class previously described. Here physical consciousness is temporarily suspended (perhaps for but a moment or so) and the Astral Body containing the consciousness of the individual is projected to some point, perhaps far distant, with the rapidity of thought, where it examines objects there situated, receiving sensations through and by means of the Astral Senses. This phenomena may arise while the person is in a trance, or sleep, etc., or else in a moment of concentrated abstraction, when one is "day-dreaming"; in a "brown study"; or "wrapped in thought." as the familiar terms run. When he returns to his physical body he "comes to himself," and what he has seen or heard seems to him like a "day-dream" or fantasy— unless he be a trained seer, in which case the two planes of consciousness will be closely related, and almost continuous.

Besides the more familiar phases of this class of phenomena, there are wonderful possibilities open for the developed Psychomancer along these lines. As a leading writer on this subject has said concerning it: "He has also the immense advantage of being able to take part, as it were, in the scenes which come before his eyes. If, in addition, he can learn how to materialize himself, he will be able to take part in physical events or conversations at a distance, and to show himself to an absent friend at will."

The trained experimenter along these lines has also the advantage of being able to search about on the Astral Plane for what he desires to find or locate. He is able to direct his Astral Body to definite places, either by means similar to finding one's way on the physical plane, or else by following up the psychic clue afforded by a piece of clothing, a lock of hair, a piece of stone, or some other object connected with the person or place desired, by means of a higher form of Psychometry. Of course, the person whose powers are not so highly developed is not able to have such control over his Astral Body, or to manifest such a degree of trained power. He is like a child learning to walk, or read—he is awkward, and must learn to direct his movements. There are many degrees of power, from the occasional, spontaneous manifestations, to those of the highly trained Occultists who travel in the Astral even more easily than in the physical, and with the same degree of certainty and control.

The pages of reliable works on Occultism and Psychic Research are filled with illustrations and examples of cases along these lines, in which the Astral Body of persons have traveled to distant scenes, and have reported occurrences and scenes witnessed there, sometimes materializing so as to be seen by the persons in the places visited. We herewith mention a few of these cases, in order to illustrate the principle.

A well-known example is that of the Philadelphian, mentioned by the German writer Jung Stilling, and quoted by some English writers. The man in question was a well-known character, respected, of good reputation and steady habits. He had the reputation of possessing Psychomantic powers which he sometimes manifested for the benefit of friends and others. He was once consulted by the wife of a sea captain, whose husband was on a voyage to Europe and Africa, and whose vessel had been long overdue, and from whom no tidings had been received for a long time.

The Psychomancer listened to the story of the anxious and distressed wife, and then excused himself from the room for a short time, retiring into an adjoining room. Becoming alarmed at his continued absence from the room, the lady quietly opened the connecting door, and peeped in the second room, where much to her surprise and alarm she saw the old man lying on a couch, showing all the appearances of death. She waited in great alarm for a long time, when he aroused himself and returned to her. He told her that he had visited her husband in a coffee-house in London, and gave her the reasons for his not having written, adding that he would soon return to Philadelphia.

When the husband finally returned, his wife questioned him regarding the matter, and he informed her that the reasons given by the Psychomancer were correct in every detail. Upon being taken into the presence of the man, the old sea captain uttered an exclamation of surprise, saying that he had seen the man on a certain day in a coffee-house in London, and that the man had told him that his wife was worried about him, and that he had answered the ma, saying that he had been prevented from writing for certain reasons, and that he was on the very eve of setting sail for America. He said that he had then lost sight of the stranger suddenly.

W. T. Stead relates the case of a lady of his acquaintance who has spontaneously developed the power to travel in her Astral Body, and to materialize the same unconsciously. She became a source of great worry and distress to many of her friends, to whom she would pay unexpected and involuntary visits, frightening them out of their wits by the materialization of what they supposed must be the "ghost" of the lady, whom they thought must have died suddenly. The occurrences, however, became so frequent that her friends at last became familiar with the nature of the appearances, and viewed them with merely great interest and wonder.

The English Society for Psychical Research have several hundred well-authenticated instances of such appearances in their published records. One of the well-known cases is that of a gentleman described as "S. H. B.," a member of the London Stock Exchange, and a man of considerable business note. He relates his story as follows:

"One Sunday night in November, 1881, I was in Kildare Gardens, when I willed very strongly that I would visit in the spirit two lady friends, the Misses V., who were living three miles off, in Hogarth Road. I willed that I should do this at one o'clock in the morning, and having willed it, I went to sleep. Next Thursday, when I first met my friends, the elder lady told me she woke up and saw my apparition advancing to her bedside. She screamed and woke her sister, who also saw me." (A signed statement of the two sisters accompanies this statement, both ladies fixing the time at one o'clock, and saying that Mr. B. wore evening dress.)

"Again, on December 1, 1882, I was at Southall. At half-past nine I sat down to endeavor to fix my mind so strongly upon the interior of a house at Kew, where Miss V. and her sister lived, that I seemed to be actually in the house. I was conscious, but was in a kind of mesmeric sleep. When I went to bed that night, I willed to be in the front bedroom of that house at Kew at twelve, and to make my presence felt by the inmates. Next day I went to Kew. Miss V.'s married sister told me, without any prompting from me, that she had seen me in the passage going from one room to another at half-past nine o'clock, and that at twelve, when she was wide awake, she saw me come to the front bedroom, where she slept, and take her hair, which is very long, into my hand. She said I then took her hand and gazed into the palm intently. She said, 'You need not look at the lines, for I never had any trouble.' She then woke her sister. When Mrs. L. told me this. I took out the entry that I had made the previous night and read it to her. Mrs. L. is quite sure she was not dreaming. She had only seen me once before, two years previously, at a fancy ball."

"Again. on March 22, 1884, I wrote to Mr. Gurney, of the Psychical Research Society, telling him I was going to make my presence felt by Miss V., at 44 Norland Square, at midnight. Ten days afterwards, I saw Miss V., when she voluntarily told me that on Saturday at midnight, she distinctly saw me, when she was quite wide awake."

We have related these accounts in order to show instances of the appearance of a materialized Astral Body. But, we must remember that these cases of materialization are very rare as compared to the cases of Astral Projection. (without materialization) in ordinary Clairvoyance. And yet the phenomena is practically the same in both instances, leaving out the phase of materialization. In many instances the individual actually travels in his Astral Body to the distant scene and there witnesses the events occurring at that point. There is a "ghost" within each one of us, which under certain favorable conditions travels away from our physical body and "sees things" at far-off points. Under certain other conditions it materializes, and is visible to others, but in the majority of cases it merely "sees" without being seen. The Psychomancer, in this phase of the phenomena, actually travels from the location of the physical body, to the other points desired, and reports what he or she sees and hears there.

Astral Projection is frequently developed by faithful practice of, and demonstration of, the simpler forms of Psychomancy. It is all a matter of successive steps of development.

LESSON VIII.

SPACE PSYCHOMANCY.

WE STATED in previous lessons, "Space Psychomancy" is the exercise of the faculty in the direction of perceiving far-distant scenes, persons, objects, etc.

Of course, there is really an exercise of Space Psychomancy in some instances of Simple Psychomancy. But we make the distinction because in the case of objects seen by Simple Psychomancy at some little distance from the observer, the impression is received by means of the rays, or vibrations from the objects themselves, by means of the developed Astral Senses, acting in a simple manner; while in the case of Space Psychomancy (in the technical sense of the term) the impression is received by means of either the erection of the Astral Tube, or else by the actual projection of the consciousness in the Astral Body—the latter being an actual visiting of the scene.

A little illustration may perhaps make clearer the above distinction. Let us suppose a man on the Physical Plane with ordinary eyesight—such a man could not see an object beyond the average distance of vision, and he would be like a person devoid of Psychomantic powers. Then let us suppose a man of extraordinary visual powers, such as many hunters or seafaring men—such a one could see things invisible to the

43

first man, and would thus resemble the person manifesting Simple Psychomancy. Then let us suppose a third man, using a telescope—this man could see things that neither of the other two could perceive, and he would thus resemble the person manifesting along the lines of Space Psychomancy by means of the Astral Tube. And, Finally let us suppose a fourth man, who possessed magical wings which would instantly transport him to the distant scene, whence he could view the objects, personally, and at close range—well this man would be like the person who was able to project his Astral Body, and thus view the distant scenes at will, and at short range, without the difficulties attendant upon the use of the telescope-like Astral Tube—to see the object on any and all sides, and from all points of view—*to get inside of it*, as well as outside.

The following interesting cases are quoted to illustrate the principle:

Captain Yount, of the Napa Valley, California, had a peculiar experience while asleep. He had a remarkably clear vision in which appeared a band of emigrants perishing from cold and hunger amidst a mountain range. He noted particularly, and in detail, the scenery and appearance of the canyon. He saw a huge, perpendicular cliff of white rock; and the emigrants cutting off what appeared to be the tops of trees arising from great drifts of snow; he even saw plainly the features of some of the party. He awoke, sorely distressed by the vividness and the nature of his "dream," for so he considered it to be. But, by-and-by, he fell asleep again, and saw the scene repeated, with equal distinctness. In the morning he found that he could not get the "dream" out of his mind, and he told it to some of his friends. One of the hearers of the story was an old hunter, who at once recognized the place seen in the dream as a place across the Sierras, known as a point in the Carson Valley Pass. So earnest was the old hunter, that Captain Yount, and his friends, organized a rescue party and set out with provisions, mules and blankets to seek the perishing emigrants. Notwithstanding the ridicule of the public, the rescuers persisted in their search, and finally about one hundred and fifty miles distant, in the Carson Valley Pass, they found the scene as described by Captain Yount, and *in the identical spot seen in the dream were found the party of emigrants*, the surviving members of whom were rescued and brought over the mountain.

Another interesting account is given in the reports of the Society for Psychical Research, of England. It relates that an English lady, Mrs. Broughton, awoke one night in 1844, and aroused her husband, telling him that she had had a strange vision of a scene in France. She stated that she had seen a broken-down carriage, evidently wrecked in an accident, and a crowd gathered around the figure of a man, whose body was then raised and carried into a nearby house. She said that the body was then placed in a bed, when she recognized his features as those of the Duke of Orleans. Then friends gathered around the bed, and later came the king and queen of France, all weeping. She saw the doctor, who stood over the Duke, feeling his pulse, with his watch in his other hand, but she could only see the doctor's back. The the scene had faded from her vision. When daylight finally came, she recorded the vision in her journal. It was before the days of the telegraph, and it was more than two days before the newspapers announced the death of the Duke of Orleans. The lady visited Paris afterward, and recognized the place of the accident. It then appeared that the attending physician whose face she could not see in her vision, was an old friend of hers, who then told her that as he watched the bed his mind had involuntarily dwelt upon her and her family.

The well-known case of Swedenborg gives us another illustration of this class of Psychomancy. It is related that in the latter part of September, 1759, at four o'clock one Saturday afternoon, Swedenborg arrived home from England, and disembarked at Gothenburg. Mr. W. Castel met him and invited him to dinner, at which meal there were fifteen persons gathered around the table. At six o'clock that evening Swedenborg went out a few minutes, returning to the table excited and pale. When questioned, he said that there was a fire at Stockholm, 200 miles distant, which was steadily spreading. He grew very restless, and frequently left the room. He said that the house of one of his friends, whose name he mentioned, was already in ashes, and that his own was in danger. At eight o'clock, after he had been out again, he returned crying out cheerfully, "Thank heaven! the fire is out, the third door from my house."

The news of the occurrence excited the whole town, and the officials made inquiry regarding it, and Swedenborg was summoned before the governor, and requested to relate what he had seen, in detail. Answering the governor, he told when and where the fire had started; how it had begun; how, when and where it had stopped; and the time it lasted, the number of houses destroyed, people injured, etc. On the following Monday morning a courier arrived from Stockholm, bringing news of the fire, having left the town while it was still burning. On the next day after, Tuesday morning, another courier arrived at the governor's palace with a full report of the fire, which corresponded precisely with the vision of Swedenborg— the fire had stopped precisely at eight o'clock, the minute that Swedenborg had so announced it to the company.

Stead relates the following instance of this class of Psychomancy, which was told him by the wife of a Dean of the Episcopal Church. The lady said: "I was staying in Virginia, some hundred miles away from home, when one morning about eleven o'clock, I felt an overpowering sleepiness, which drowsiness was quite unusual, and which caused me to lie down. In my sleep I saw quite distinctly my home in Richmond in flames. The fire had broken out in one wing of the house, which I saw with dismay was where I kept all my best dresses. The people were all trying to check the flames, but it was no use. My husband was there, walking about before the burning house, carrying a portrait in his hand. Everything was quite clear and distinct, exactly as if I had actually been present and seen everything. After a time, I woke up, and going downstairs told my friends the strange dream I had had. They laughed at me, and made such game of my vision that I did my best to think no more about it. I was traveling about, a day or two passed, and when Sunday came I found myself in a church where some relatives were worshipping. When I entered the pew they looked rather strange, and as soon as the service was over I asked them what was the matter. 'Don't be alarmed,' they said, 'there is nothing serious.' Then they handed me a postcard from my husband which simply said, 'House burned out; covered by insurance.' *The day was the date upon which my dream occurred.* I hastened home, and then I learned that everything had happened exactly as I had seen it. The fire had broken out in the wing I had seen blazing. My clothes were all burnt, and the oddest thing about it was that my husband, having rescued a favorite picture from the burning building, had carried it about among the crowd for some time before he could find a place in which to put it safely."

A well-authenticated case is that of the wreck of the ship "Strathmore." Stead relates the story as follows: "The father of a son who had sailed in the 'Strathmore,' an emigrant ship outbound from the Clyde, saw one night the ship foundering amid the waves, and saw that his son, with some others, had escaped safely to a desert island near which the wreck had taken place. He was so much impressed by this vision that he wrote to the owner of the 'Strathmore,' telling him what he had seen. His information was scouted; but after a while the 'Strathmore' became overdue, and the owner became uneasy. Day followed day, and still no tidings of the missing ship. Then, like Pharaoh's butler, the owner remembered his sins one day, and hunted up the letter describing the vision. It supplied at least a theory to account for the vessel's disappearance. All outward-bound ships were requested to look out for any survivors on the island indicated in the vision. These orders being obeyed, the survivors of the 'Strathmore' were found exactly where the father had seen them."

Another interesting case is reported by the Society previously mentioned. It reports that Dr. Golinski, a physician of Kremeutchug. Russia, was taking an after-dinner nap in the afternoon, about half-past three o'clock. He had a vision in which he saw himself called out on a professional visit, which took him to a little room with dark hangings. To the right of the door he saw a chest of drawers, upon which rested a little paraffine lamp of special pattern, different from anything he had ever seen before. On the left of the door, he saw a woman suffering from a severe hemorrhage. He then saw himself giving her professional treatment. Then he awoke, suddenly, and saw that it was just half-past four o'clock. Then comes the strange sequel. Within ten minutes after he awoke, he was called out on a professional visit, and on entering the bedroom he saw all the details that had appeared to him in his vision. There was the chest of drawers—there was the peculiar lamp—there was the woman on the bed suffering from the hemorrhage. Upon inquiry he found that she had grown worse between three and four o'clock, and had anxiously desired that he come to her about that time, finally dispatching a messenger for him at half-past four, the moment at which he awoke.

We could fill page after page with these interesting and well-authenticated instances, but our lack of space prevents. We have stated enough to illustrate the principle, and then, besides, many of our readers will know of many similar instances in the actual experience of themselves, relatives or friends. Volumes would not contain all the true stories of phenomena of this kind—and still people smile in a superior way at the mere suggestion of the phenomena.

LESSON IX.

PAST TIME PSYCHOMANCY.

A W WE have previously stated, "Time Psychomancy" is a term used to designate that phase of the phenomena in which one senses objects, events, persons, etc., in the records of the past; and also in which he senses the indications of the future—"the shadows of coming events."

For convenience, we shall separate our consideration of the subject into two parts, viz.: (1) Past Time Psychomancy; and (2) Future Time Psychomancy.

Past Time Psychomancy is that phase of the phenomena which enables one to use his Astral Vision to explore the records of the past, and we shall now proceed to examine.

The first question that naturally arises in the minds of careful students, in connection with this phase of the phenomena, is, "How is the person able to sense the scenes, occurrences, and objects of the past? There are no vibrations emanating from past scenes, and as they no longer exist, how can anyone see them, by Astral Vision, or by any other means?" This question is a most proper one, for even those who readily grasp the explanation of Space Psychomancy find themselves at a loss to understand the Past Time phenomena without a knowledge of the Occult Teachings on the subjects.

49

THE AKASHIC RECORDS.

The secret of Past Time Psychomancy is found in the Occult Teaching of the "Akashic Records," by which is meant that on the higher planes of Universal Substance, there are to be found records of all that has happened and occurred during the entire World Cycle of which the present time forms a part. These records are preserved until the termination of the World Cycle, when they pass away with the World of which they are a record. This does not mean that there is any Great Book in which the doings, good and bad, of people are written down by the Recording Angel, as popular fanciful legends has it. But it does mean that there is a scientific occult basis for the popular legend, in spite of the sneers of the skeptics. We must turn to modern science for a corroboration. It is now taught by scientists that there is no such thing as a destruction of Energy, but that Energy always exists in some form. The Occult Teachings verify this, and go further, when they state that every action, thought, happening, event. occurrence, etc., no matter how small or insignificant, leaves an indelible record on the Akasha (or Universal Ether) with which Space is filled. In other words, every action, or scene, that has ever occurred or existed in the past, has left an impression in the Universal Ether, or Akasha, where it may be read by developed Psychomancy.

There is nothing especially wonderful about this, when you compare it with other facts in nature. Astronomy teaches us that light travels at the rate of 186,000 miles a sccond—and that there are fixed stars in space so far removed from the Earth that their light leaving them hundreds, yes, thousands, of years ago, is only now reaching our sight. In other words, when we look at some of the fixed stars, we do not see them as they now are, or where they now are, but merely see them where and how they were hundreds of years ago when the rays of light left them. Astronomers tell us that if one of these stars happened to be blotted out of existence hundreds of years ago, we would be still seeing the light that left them before the event—in other words would be seeing them hundreds of years after they had ceased to be. And our children, and children's children, for several generations would still see them, and would not learn of the terrible catastrophe for hundreds of years after it actually happened. The vibrations of light once set into motion would persist for centuries, and even for thousands of years after their source had disappeared. This is no wild occult fancy, but a well-proven and thoroughly-established scientific fact, as anyone may see for himself by reference to any work on astronomy. And the same is true of waves of electricity, or electronic emanations, or waves of any kind of energy. Really, even in the physical view of things, nothing can exist without leaving a record in the Universal Ether. And so the Occult Teachings now find their corroboration in Modern Science.

Another illustration is found in the phenomena of the Memory of Man. Stored away in our brain-cells are records of things, events, scenes, occurrences, people, and objects, registered there in past years. You often find yourself thinking about people, things and events of years long since passed away—and by a mere effort of the will you bring the records of these people, things, or events before your mental vision and see them reproduced in detail. Dissect a brain-cell and you will find no trace of the thing there—but nevertheless every exercise of memory proves that the record is there. And there is nothing more wonderful, or miraculous, in the Akashic Records of Past Events, than there is in the Memory Record of Past Events! The Universal Ether, or Akasha, has within itself a true and full record of anything, and everything, that has ever existed within its space. And if one develops the power to read these records at will, he has a full and complete key to the past, from the speaking of the Creative Word which began this great World Cycle.

But, in order to avoid a misapprehension, we must say to our students that none but the most advanced and highly-developed Occultists and Masters have clear access to the planes upon which these records are to be found. The majority of Psychomancers merely see on the "Lower Astral Plane" a reflection of the Akashic Records, which reflection may be compared to the reflection of the trees and landscape in a pond of water, which, of course, is often more or less imperfect—distorted and disturbed by the ripples and waves occasioned by the passing breezes, and sometimes being made muddy and clouded. The records of the Past, open to the average Psychomancer, are merely "*reflections of records,*" which are apt to be more or less distorted, or cloudy, by reason of the disturbances of the surface of the reflecting medium. This is a brief and simple statement of an important Occult scientific truth, which would require volumes to explain technically. The illustration of the reflecting surface of the water, however, is so true to the real facts that the student may confidently adopt the same as his mental image of the phenomena of Past Time Psychomancy.

In actual practice we find the phenomena of Past Time Psychomancy manifested principally along the line of Psychometry and Crystal Gazing, the consideration of which phases of phenomena has been made in previous lessons in this book. There are to be found, however, many instances of at least a partial manifestation of this phase of power among individuals in every-day life, who when meeting a person frequently get impressions (more or less correct) of his or her past life, past scenes, etc.

The German writer, Zschokke, in his autobiography, writes as follows regarding this power of Past Time Psychomancy possessed by him, and which was often set into operation when he came into the presence of strangers for the first time. He states: "It has happened to me sometimes, on my first meeting with strangers, as I silently listened to their discourse, that their former life, with many trifling circumstances therewith connected, or frequently some particular scene in that life, has passed quite involuntarily, and, as it were, dream-like, yet perfectly distinct, before me. During this time I usually feel so entirely absorbed in the contemplation of the stranger's life, that at last I no longer see clearly the face of the unknown wherein I undesignedly read, nor distinctly hear the voices of the speakers, which before served in some measure as a commentary on the text of their features. For a long time I held such visions as delusions of the fancy, and the more so as they showed me even the dress and emotions of the actors, rooms, furniture, and other accessories, but I soon discovered otherwise."

"On one occasion, in a gay mood, I narrated to my family the secret history of a seamstress who had just before quitted the room. I had never seen the young woman before. Nevertheless, the hearers were astonished and laughed, and would not be persuaded but that O had a previous acquaintance with her and the facts of her former life, inasmuch as what I had stated was perfectly true. I was not the less astonished than they to find that my vision agreed with reality."

"I then gave more attention to the subject, and as often as propriety allowed of it, I related to those whose lives had passed before me, the substance of my visions, in order to obtain from them a contradiction or verification thereof. On every occasion the confirmation followed, not without amazement on the part of those who gave it."

"One day, in the city of Waldshut, I entered an inn (the Vine) in company with two young students. We supped with a numerous company at the table d'hote, where the guests were making very merry with the peculiarities of the Swiss, with Mesmer's magnetism. Lavater's physiognomy, etc. One of my companions, whose national pride was wounded by their mockery, begged me to make some reply, particularly to a handsome young man who sat opposite to us, and who had allowed himself extraordinary license. This man's life was at that moment presented to my mind. I turned to him, and asked whether he would answer me candidly if I related to him some of the most secret passages of his life, I knowing as little of him personally as he did of me. He promised, if I were correct, to admit it frankly. I then related what my vision had shown me, and the whole company were made acquainted with the private history of the young merchant—his school years. his youthful errors, and, lastly, with a fault committed in reference to the strong-box of his principal. I described the uninhabited room with whitened walls, where, to the right of the brown door, on a table, stood a black money-box, etc. A dead silence prevailed during the whole narrative, which I alone occasionally interrupted by inquiring whether I spoke the truth. The startled young man confirmed every particular, and even, what I had scarcely expected, the last mentioned. Touched by his candor, I shook hands with him, and said no more. He is, probably, still living."

LESSON X.

FUTURE TIME PSYCHOMANCY.

"**F**UTURE TIME Psychomancy," as the term itself indicates, is the name given to that class of the phenomena in which one is able to sense the Astral Plane impression of coming events—the psychic shadows thrown before by coming events. In order to give the student a technical nature of the occult cause behind this phenomena would require volumes of the deepest metaphysical lore, which field is foreign to the purposes of this work which deals with phenomena alone, and does not enter into the metaphysical side of the subject.

It will be sufficient for the student to understand that in the Astral as well as on the Physical Plane, "*Coming Events cast their Shadows Before.*" Without entering into a discussion of Destiny or Fate, or anything of that kind, it may be stated that *when Causes are set into motion, the Effects follow,* unless other Causes intervene. In some cases certain effects have been averted by reason of the previous Vision—in such cases *the other Causes intervened,* which showed that the matter was not wholly "cut and dried." It is like a man walking toward a precipice—he will walk over unless he is warned in some way. He is not "fated" to walk over but over he will go, unless warned and prevented. Do you see what we mean?

On the other hand, there seem to be cases in which the person seems unable to escape the Effect of Causes once set into motion—he even seems to run into the effect, while seeking to escape it. In this connection the little fable of the Persians may be quoted. The story goes that a friend was with Solomon when the Angel of Death entered and gazed at him fixedly. Upon learning who the strange visitor was, the friend said to Solomon, "Pray transport me on thy magic carpet to Damascus, that I may escape this dread messenger." And Solomon complied with his request, and the man was instantly magically transported to Damascus. Then said the Angel of Death to Solomon: "O Solomon, the reason that I gazed so intently at thy friend was because I had orders from On High to take him from the body at Damascus, and lo! finding him here at Jerusalem, I was sore perplexed as to how to obey my orders. But, thou, by transporting him to Damascus hath rendered my task an easy one. Many thanks, for thy help at thy friend's suggestion, O King!" And saying which the Angel of Death was wafted away to Damascus to take the man, according to orders.

The phenomena of Premonitions, Prevision, and Second Sight, are all forms or phases of Future Time Psychomancy. In these various forms the phenomena is of quite common and frequent occurrence, and is met with all over the world. In the Isle of Skye many persons possess the gift of Second Sight in varying degree, but they claim that a native of the island loses the power when he moves to the mainland. In the same way the Scotch Highlander (among whose people the gift is quite common) is said to sometimes lose the faculty when he removes to the lowlands. The Westphalian peasants also are noted for the power of Second Sight.

An instance of this phase of the phenomena, well known in England, is that connected with the assassination of Mr. Percival in the lobby of the House of Commons. This deed was foreseen by John Williams, a Cornish mine manager, some nine days before its actual occurrence, the vision being perfect down to the most minute details. Williams had the vision three times in succession. He saw a small man, dressed in a blue coat and white waistcoat, enter the lobby of the House of Commons, when another person, dressed in a snuff-colored coat, stepped forward and drawing a pistol from an inside pocket fire at and shot the little man, the bullet lodging in the left breast. He seemed to ask some bystander who was the victim, and he received the reply that it was Mr. Percival, the Chancellor of the Exchequer. Williams was so much wrought up over the vision, that he seriously contemplated going to London to warn the victim, but his friends, to whom he told the story, ridiculed him and persuaded him not to go on "a fool's errand." A few days later the news was received of the assassination of Mr. Percival, in precisely the manner indicated by the vision.

George Fox, the Quaker, experienced the impression of "a waft of death" about Cromwell when he met him riding at Hampton Court, shortly before his fatal illness. Fox also foretold the expulsion of the "Rump Parliament;" the restoration of Charles II; and the Fire of London. Caesar's wife had a warning of her husband's death. The Bible is filled with similar instances.

We will conclude this lesson with a recital of the wonderful instance of Cazotte, whose prediction, and its literal fulfilment, are now matters of French history. La Harpe tells the story as follows:

"It appears but as yesterday, and yet, nevertheless, it was at the beginning of the year 1788. We were dining with one of our brethren at the Academy—a man of considerable wealth and genius. The conversation became serious; much admiration was expressed on the revolution in thought which Voltaire had effected, and it was agreed that it was his first claim to the reputation he enjoyed. We concluded that the revolution must soon be consummated; that it was indispensable that superstition and fanaticism should give place to philosophy, and we began to calculate the probability of the period when this should be, and which of the present company should live to see it. The oldest complained that they could scarcely flatter themselves with the hope; the younger rejoiced that they might entertain this very probable expectation; and they congratulated the Academy especially for having prepared this great work, and for having been the great rallying point, the centre, and the prime mover of the liberty of thought.

"One only of the guests had not taken part in all the joyousness of this conversation, and had gently and cheerfully checked our splendid enthusiasm. This was Cazotte, an amiable and original man, but unhappily infatuated with the reveries of the illuminati. He spoke, and with the most serious tone. 'Gentlemen,' said he, 'be satisfied; you will all see this great and sublime revolution, which you so much desire. You know that I am a little inclined to prophesy; I repeat, you will see it.' He was answered by the common rejoinder: 'One need not be a conjuror to see that.' 'Be it so; but perhaps one must be a little more than conjuror for what remains for me to tell you. Do you know what will be the consequence of this revolution—what will be consequence to all of you, and what will be the immediate result—the well-established effect— the thoroughly-recognized consequence to all of you who are here present?' 'Ah!' said Condorcet, with his insolent and half-suppressed smile, 'let us hear—a philosopher is not sorry to encounter a prophet.' 'You, Monsieur de Condorcet—you will yield up your last breath on the floor of a dungeon; you will die from poison, which you will have taken, in order to escape from execution—from poison which the happiness of that time will oblige you to carry about your person.'

"'Monsieur de Chamfort, you will open your veins with twenty-two cuts of a razor, and yet you will not die till some months afterward.' They looked at each other, and laughed again. 'You, Monsieur Vicq d'Azir, you will not open your own veins, but you will cause yourself to be bled six times in one day, during a paroxysm of the gout, in order to make more sure of your end, and you will die in the night. You, Monsieur de Nicolai, you will die upon the scaffold; you, Monsieur Bailly, on the scaffold; you, Monsieur de Malesherbes, on the scaffold.' 'Ah! God be thanked,' exclaimed Roucher, 'and what of I?' 'You! you also will die upon the scaffold' 'Yes.' replied Chamfort. 'but when will all this happen?' 'Six years will not pass over, before all that I have said to you shall be accomplished.'

"'Here are some astonishing miracles (and, this time, it was I myself (La Harpe) who spoke), but you have not included me in your list.' 'But you will be there, as an equally extraordinary miracle; you will then be a Christian.' Vehement exclamation on all sides. 'Ah,' replied Chamfort, 'I am comforted; if we shall perish only when La Harpe shall be a Christian, we are immortal.'

"'As for that,' then observed Madame la Duchesse de Grammont, 'we women, we are happy to be counted for nothing in these revolutions: when I say for nothing, it is not that we do not always mix ourselves up with them a little; but it is a received maxim that they take no notice of us, and of our sex.' 'Your sex, ladies, will not protect you this time; and you had far better meddle with nothing, for you will be treated entirely as men, without any difference whatever.' 'But what, then, are you really telling us of, Monsieur Cazotte? You are preaching to us the end of the world.' 'I know nothing on this subject; but what I do know is, that you, Madame la Duchesse, will be conducted to the scaffold, you and many other ladies with you, in the cart of the executioner, and with your hands tied behind your backs.' 'Ah! I hope that, in that case, I shall at least have a carriage hung in black.' 'No, madame; higher ladies than yourself will go, like you, in the common car, with their hands tied behind them.' 'Higher ladies! what! the princesses of the blood?' 'Still more exalted personages.' Here a sensible emotion pervaded the whole company, and the countenance of the host was dark and lowering; they began to feel that the joke was become too serious.

"Madame de Grammont, in order to dissipate the cloud, took no notice of the reply, and contented herself with saying in a careless tone: 'You see that he will not leave me even a confessor!' 'No, madame, you will not have one—neither you, nor anyone besides. The last victim to whom this favor will be afforded will be——' He stopped for a moment. 'Well! who then will be the happy mortal to whom this prerogative will be given?' ''Tis the only one which he will have then retained—and that will be the king of France.'"

The amazing sequel to this historical prediction is that *it was verified in every detail*, as all students of the French Revolution know—*and all within the six years*, as Cazotte foretold.

Lesson XI.

Dream Psychomancy.

THE STUDENT will have noted that in many cases mentioned in these lessons, the Psychomantic vision manifested during physical sleep. The reason of this occurrence is that in the majority of persons the physical nature, when awake, holds the attention of the individual to such an extent as to prevent him from manifesting the psychic faculties clearly. But when the physical body sinks into sleep then the field is clear for the exercise of the Astral Senses, which not being fatigued, are in fine condition to manifest. In fact the majority of persons do manifest Psychomancy during sleep, but have little or no recollection of the same when waking, beyond indistinct recollections of "dreams," etc. Still, many of you who read these lines will have a more or less clear remembrance of certain "dreams" in which you seemed to visit other places, scenes, lands, countries, etc., seeing strange faces, landscapes, etc., and upon awakening were somewhat anoyed at having been brought back from your pleasant travels.

It is not our intention to enter into an extended consideration of the general subject of Dreams, at this time and place. We write these few lines merely for the purpose of calling your attention to the fact that the phenomena of Psychomancy very frequently manifests itself in Dreams, for the reasons stated above. The principle in both the waking and dream phenomena is precisely the same, the apparent difference being that the dreamer very seldom carries back with him a clear and connected memory of his vision, while the waking person is able to impress his Astral vision upon a wide-awake physical brain, there to be remembered.

You will find several instances of Dream Psychomancy recorded in the various lessons of this work, inserted for the purpose of illustrating the several phases of the phenomena. In such cases we have made no distinction between the Psychomantic phenomena experienced in dreams on the one hand, and that experienced in the waking state on the other hand. The principle is the same in both cases, and there is no necessity for making any such distinction between the phenomena occurring under any of the several general classes. But as we still have to spare a few pages of the space allotted to us in the preparation of these lessons, we think that we should give you a few more of the many interesting cases of record.

A well-known and interesting case is that mentioned in the Proceedings of the Psychical Research Society, of London. It is related as follows:

On September 9th, 1848, at the siege of Mooltan, Major-General R. was most severely and dangerously wounded; and, supposing himself to be dying, asked one of the officers with him to take the ring off his finger and send it to his wife, who a time was fully 150 miles distant at Ferozepore.

"On the night of September 9th, 1848," writes his wife, "I was lying on my bed, between sleeping and waking, when I distinctly saw my husband being carried off the field seriously wounded, and heard his voice, saying, 'Take this ring off my finger and send it to my wife.' All the next day I could not get the sight or the voice out of my mind. In due time I heard of General R. having been seriously wounded in the assault of Mooltan. He survived, however, and is still living. It was not for some time after the siege that I heard from General L., the officer who helped to carry my husband off the field, that the request as to the ring was actually made by him, just as I heard it at Ferozepore at that very time."

The following, related by Mrs. Crowe, is interesting, particularly in its aspect as a warning:

"A few years ago, Dr. Watson, now residing at Glasgow, dreamt that he received a summons to attend a patient at a place some miles from where he was living; that he started on horseback, and that as he was crossing a moor, he saw a bull making furiously at him, whose horns he escaped only by taking refuge on a spot inaccessible to the animal, where he waited a long time till some people, observing his situation, came to his assistance and released him. While at breakfast the following morning the summons came, and smiling at the odd coincidence (as he thought it), he started on horseback. He was quite ignorant of the road he had to go, but by and by he arrived at the moor, which he recognized, and presently the bull appeared, coming full tilt towards him. But his dream had shown him the place of refuge, for which he instantly made, and there he spent three or four hours besieged by the animal, till the country people set him free. Dr. Watson declared that but for the dream he should not have known in what direction to run for safety."

This case is an instance of Future Time Psychomancy, as the student will readily see. Here is another case coming under the same classification. It is related by Dr. Lee:

Mrs. Hannah Green, the housekeeper of a country family in Oxfordshire, dreamt one night that she had been left alone in the house on a Sunday evening, and that hearing a knock at the door of the chief entrance, she went to it and found confronting her an ugly tramp, armed with a big club, who forced himself into the house in spite of her struggles, striking her insensible with his club during the conflict. She awoke at this point. A considerable period of time elapsed, and she had almost forgotten her dream until it was recalled in a startling manner. She was then in charge of an isolated mansion at Kensington, and on a Sunday afternoon, when the servants had taken a holiday, leaving her alone, she was startled by a loud knock at the door. At once the memory of her dream flashed before her, with singular vividness and remarkable force. She knew that she was alone, but for the purpose of frightening away the intruder she lighted a lamp on the ball table, and afterward in other places in the house, and also rang the bells violently in different parts of the house. She also made sure that the doors and windows were fastened. She succeeded in scaring off the man, by making him believe that the house was occupied by the family, or several people at least, but not until she had thrown up the window over the stair landing, and there to her intense terror saw the identical man of her dream, armed with the same club, and demanding an entrance. Had she not been warned by the dream of several years previous, she would have met with a fate such as she had dreamed of.

The following case of Dream Psychomancy, which is a good example of Astral Projection during sleep, is related by a correspondent of the Psychical Research Society, as follows:

"One morning in December, 1836, he had the following dream, or, he would prefer to call it, revelation. He found himself suddenly at the gate of Major N. M.'s avenue, many miles from his home. Close to him was a group of persons, one of whom was a woman with a basket on her arm, the rest men, four of whom were tenants of his own, while the others were unknown to him. Some of the strangers seemed to be assaulting H. W., one of his tenants, and he interfered. 'I struck violently at the man on my left, and then with greater violence at the man's face on my right. Finding, to my surprise, that I had not knocked down either, I struck again and again with all the violence of a man frenzied at the sight of my poor friend's murder. To my great amazement I saw my arms, although visible to my eye, were without substance, and the bodies of the men I struck at and my own came close together after each blow through the shadowy arms I struck with. My blows were delivered with more extreme violence than I ever think I exerted, but I became painfully convinced of my incompetency. I have no consciousness of what happened after this feeling of unsubstantiality came upon me.' Next morning A. experienced the stiffness and soreness of violent bodily exercise, and was informed by his wife that in the course of the night he had much alarmed her by striking out again and again with his arms in a terrific manner, 'as if fighting for his life.' He, in turn, informed her of his dream, and begged her to remember the names of those actors in it who were known to him. On the morning of the following day (Wednesday) A. received a letter from his agent, who resided in the town close to the scene of the dream, informing him that his tenant had been found on Tuesday morning at Major N. M.'s gate, speechless and apparently dying from a fracture of the skull, and that there was no trace of the murderers. That night A. started for the town, and arrived there on Thursday morning. On his way to a meeting of magistrates he met the senior magistrate of that part of the country, and requested him to give orders for the arrest of the three men whom, besides H. W., he had recognized in his dream, and to have them examined separately. This was at once done. The three men gave identical accounts of the occurrence, and all named the woman who was with them. She was then arrested, and gave precisely similar testimony. They said that between eleven and twelve on the Monday night they had been walking homewards altogether along the road, when they were overtaken by three strangers, two of whom savagely assaulted H. W., while the other prevented his friends from interfering. H. W. did not die, but was never the same man afterwards; he subsequently emigrated"

Stead relates the following case, which was imparted to him as a truthful and correct account of the vision of a murder seen in all of its details by a brother of the murdered man. It is a case of Astral Projection, undoubtedly:

"St.Eglos is situated about ten miles from the Atlantic, and not quite so far from the old market town of Trebodwina. Hart and George Northey were brothers, and from childhood their lives had been marked by the strongest brotherly affection. Hart and George Northey had never been separated from their birth until George became a sailor, Hart meantime joining his father in business. On the 8th of February, 1840, while George Northey's ship was lying in port at St. Helena, he had the following strange dream:

"'Last night I dreamt my brother was at Trebodwina Market, and that I was with him, quite close by his side, during the whole of the market transactions. Although I could see and hear everything which passed around me, I felt sure that it was not my bodily presence which thus accompanied him, but my shadow, or rather my spiritual presence, for he seemed quite unconscious that I was near him. I felt that my being thus present in this strange way betokened some hidden danger which he was destined to meet, and which I knew my presence could not avert, for I could not speak to warn him of his peril.'"

The brother having collected considerable money then started on his ride homeward. The story then continues:

"'My terror gradually increased as Hart approached the hamlet of Polkerrow, until I was in a perfect frenzy, frantically desirous, yet unable, to warn my brother in some way and prevent him going further. I suddenly became aware of two dark shadows thrown across the road. I felt my brother's hour had come, and I was powerless to aid him! Two men appeared, whom I instantly recognized as notorious poachers, who lived in a lonely wood near St. Eglos. The men wished him "Good-night," maister," civilly enough. He replied, and entered into conversation with them about some work he had promised them. After a few minutes they asked him for some money. The elder of the two brothers, who was standing near the horse's head, said,

"Mr. Northey, we know you have just come from Trebodwina market with plenty of money in your pockets; we are desperate men, and you bean't going to leave this place until we've got that money, so hand over." My brother made no reply, except to slash at him with the whip and spur the horse at him.

"'The younger of the ruffians instantly drew a pistol and fired. Hart dropped lifeless from the saddle, and one of the villains held him by the throat with a grip of iron for some minutes, as though to make assurance doubly sure, and crush out any particle of life my poor brother might have left. The murderers secured the horse to a tree in the orchard, and, having rifled the corpse, they dragged it up the stream, concealing it under the overhanging banks of the water-course. They then carefully covered over all marks of blood on the road, and hid the pistol in the thatch of a disused hut close to the roadside; then, setting the horse free to gallop home alone, they decamped across the country to their own cottage.'

"The vessel left St. Helena next day, and reached Plymouth in due course. George Northey had, during the whole of the voyage home, never altered his conviction that Hart had been killed as he had dreamt, and that retribution was by his means to fall on the murderers."

The sequel shows that the murder was actually committed in precisely the manner in which it had appeared to the brother in the dream. The crime aroused universal horror and indignation, and every effort was made to discover the murderers and bring them to justice. Two brothers named Hightwood were suspected, and a search of their cottage revealed blood-stained garments, but no trace of the pistol was to be found, although the younger brother admitted having had one and lost it.' The story continues:

"Both brothers were arrested and brought before the magistrates. The evidence against them was certainly not strong, but their manner seemed that of guilty men. They were ordered to take their trial at the forthcoming assizes at Trebodwina.

They each confessed in the hope of saving their lives, and both were sentenced to be hanged. There was, however, some doubt about the pistol. Before the execution George Northey arrived from St. Helena, and declared that the pistol was in the thatch of the old cottage close by the place where they murdered Hart Northey, and where they hid it. 'How did you know?' he was asked. George Northey replied: 'I saw the foul deed committed in a dream I had the night of the murder, when at St. Helena.' A pistol was found, as George Northey had predicted, in the thatch of the ruined cottage."

We trust that we have established the identity of Waking Psychomancy, and Dream Psychomancy, to your satisfaction.

FINIS.

BIBLIOGRAPHY

Atkinson, William Walker. *Practical Psychomancy and Crystal Gazing: A Course of Lessons on the Psychic Phenomena of Distant Sensing, Clairvoyance, Psychometry, Crystal Gazing, Etc. Containing Practical Instruction, Exercises, Directions, etc., capable of being understood, mastered and demonstrated by any person of average intelligence.* Chicago, IL: The Fiduciary Press, 1907.

Atkinson, William Walker. *Practical Psychomancy and Crystal Gazing: A Course of Lessons on the Psychic Phenomena of Distant Sensing, Clairvoyance, Psychometry, Crystal Gazing, Etc. Containing Practical Instruction, Exercises, Directions, etc., capable of being understood, mastered and demonstrated by any person of average intelligence.* Chicago, IL: Advanced Thought Puplishing Co., 1908.

Leadbetter, C. W. *Clairvoyance.* London, GB: The Theosophical Publishing Society., 1899.

Page 40, 41, 42, 46,47, 52, 53, 54, 58, 59, 60, 62, 63, 64-66, 68, 69, 70-74

MENTAL SCIENCE

I have spoken to you of the advantage of getting rid of Fear. Now I wish to put LIFE into you. Many of you have been going along as if you were dead - no ambition - no energy - no vitality - no interest - no life. This will never do. You are stagnating. Wake up and display a few signs of life! This is not the place in which you can stalk around like a living corpse - this is the place for wide-awake, active, live people, and a good general awakening is what is needed; although it would take nothing less than a blast from Gabriel's trumpet to awaken some of the people who are stalking around thinking that they are alive, but who are really dead to all that makes life worthwhile.

We must let Life flow through us, and allow it to express itself naturally. Do not let the little worries of life, or the big ones either, depress you and cause you to lose your vitality. Assert the Life Force within you, and manifest it in every thought, act and deed, and before long you will be exhilarated and fairly bubbling over with vitality and energy.

Put a little life into your work - into your pleasures - into yourself. Stop doing things in a half-headed way, and begin to take an interest in what you are doing, saying and thinking. It is astonishing how much interest we may find in the ordinary things of life if we will only wake up. There are interesting things all around us - interesting events occurring every moment - but we will not be aware of them unless we assert our life force and begin to actually live instead of merely existing.

No man or woman ever amounted to anything unless he or she put life into the tasks of everyday life - the acts - the thoughts. What the world needs is live men and women. Just look into the eyes of the people whom you meet, and see how few of them are really alive. The most of them lack that expression of conscious life which distinguishes the man who lives from the one who simply exists.

Develop Your Latent Paranormal Powers

I want you to acquire this sense of conscious life so that you may manifest it in your life and show what Mental Science has done for you. I want you to get to work today and begin to make yourselves over according to the latest pattern. You can do this if you will only take the proper interest in the task.

Fix in your mind the thought that the "I" within you is very much alive and that you are manifesting life fully, mentally and physically. And keep this though there, aiding yourself with constant repetitions of the watchword. Don't let the thought escape you, but keep pushing it back into the mind. Keep it before the mental vision as much as possible. Repeat the watchword when you awaken in the morning - say it when you retire at night. And say it at meal times, and whenever else you can during the day - at least once an hour. Form the mental picture of yourself as filled with Life and Energy. Live up to it as far as possible. When you start in to perform a task say "I AM Alive" and mix up as much life as possible in the task. If you find yourself feeling depressed, say "I AM Alive," and then take a few deep breaths, and with each inhalation let the mind hold the thought that you are breathing in Strength and Life, and as you exhale, hold the thought that you are breathing out all the old, dead, negative conditions and are glad to get rid of them. Then finish up with an earnest, vigorous affirmation: "I AM Alive," and mean it when you say it too.

And let your thoughts take form in action. Don't rest content with merely saying that you are alive, but prove it with your acts. Take an interest in doing things, and don't go around "mooning" or daydreaming. Get down to business, and LIVE.

PROFESSOR William James, the well-known teacher of, and writer upon Psychology very truly says: "The great thing in all education is to make our nervous system our ally instead of our enemy. For this we must make automatic and habitual, as early as possible, as many useful actions as we can and as carefully guard against growing into ways that are likely to be disadvantageous. In the acquisition of a new habit, or the leaving off of an old one we must take care to launch ourselves with as strong and decided initiative as possible. Never suffer an exception to occur until the new habit is securely rooted in your life. Seize the very first possible opportunity to act on every resolution you make and on every emotional prompting you may experience, in the direction of the habits you aspire to gain."

This advice is along the lines familiar to all students of Mental Science, but it states the matter more plainly than the majority of us have done. It impresses upon us the importance of passing on to the subconscious mind the proper impulses, so that they will become automatic and "second nature." Our subconscious mentality is a great storehouse for all sorts of suggestions from ourselves and others and, as it is the "habit-mind," we must be careful to send it the proper material from which it may make habits. If we get into the habit of doing certain things, we may be sure that the subconscious mentality will make it easier for us to do just the same thing over and over again, easier each time, until finally we are firmly bound with the ropes and chains of the habit, and find it more or less difficult, sometimes almost impossible, to free ourselves from the hateful thing.

We should cultivate good habits against the hour of need. The time will come when we will be required to put forth our best efforts, and it rests with us today whether that hour of need shall find us doing the proper thing automatically and almost without thought, or struggling to do it bound down and hindered with the chains of things opposed to that which we desire at that moment.

We must be on guard at all times to prevent the forming of undesirable habits. There may be no special harm in doing a certain thing today, or perhaps again tomorrow, but there may be much harm in setting up the habit of of doing that particular thing. If you are confronted with the question: "Which of these two things should I do?" the best answer is: "I will do that which I would like to become a habit with me."

In forming a new habit, or in breaking an old one, we should throw ourselves into the task with as much enthusiasm as possible, in order to gain the most ground before the energy expends itself when it meets with friction from the opposing habits already formed. We should start in by making as strong an impression as possible upon the subconscious mentality. Then we should be constantly on guard against temptations to break the new resolution "just this once." This "just once" idea kills off more good resolutions than any other one cause. The moment you yield "just this once, you introduce the thin edge of the wedge that will, in the end, split your resolution into pieces.

Equally important is the fact that each time you resist temptation the stronger does your resolution become. Act upon your resolution as early and as often as possible, as with every manifestation of thought in action, the stronger does it become. You are adding to the strength of your original resolution every time you back it up with action.

The mind has been likened to a piece of paper that has been folded. Ever afterwards it has a tendency to fold in the same crease - unless we make a new crease or fold, when it will follow the last lines. And the creases are habits - every time we make one it is so much easier for the mind to fold along the same crease afterward. Let us make our mental creases in the right direction.

ONE is apt to think of the emotions as independent from habit. We easily may think of one acquiring habits of action, and even of thinking, but we are apt to regard the emotions as something connected with "feeling" and quite divorced from intellectual effort. Yet, notwithstanding the distinction between the two, both are dependent largely upon habit, and one may repress, increase, develop, and change one's emotions, just as one may regulate habits of action and lines of thought.

It is an axiom of psychology that "Emotions deepen by repetition." If a person allows a state of feeling to thoroughly take possession of him, he will find it easier to yield to the same emotion the second time, and so on, until the particular emotion or feeling becomes second nature to him. If an undesirable emotion shows itself inclined to take up a permanent abode with you, you had better start to work to get rid of it, or at least to master it. And the best time to do this is at the start; for each repetition renders the habit more firmly entrenched, and the task of dislodging it more difficult.

Were you ever jealous? If so, you will remember how insidious was its first approach; how subtly it whispered hateful suggestions into your willing ear, and how gradually it followed up such suggestions, until, finally you began to see green. (Jealousy has an effect upon the bile, and causes it to poison the blood. This is why the idea of green is always associated with it.) Then you will remember how the thing seemed to grow, taking possession of you until you scarcely could shake it off. You found it much easier to become jealous the next time. It seemed to bring before you all sorts of objects apparently justifying your suspicions and feeling. Everything began to look green - the green-eyed monster waxed fat.

And so it is with every feeling or emotion. If you give way to a fit of rage, you will find it easier to become angry the next time, on less provocation. The habit of feeling and acting "mean" does not take long to firmly settle itself in its new home if encouraged. Worry is a great habit for growing and waxing fat. People start by worrying about big things, and then begin to worry and fret about some smaller thing. And then the merest trifle worries and distresses them. They imagine that all sorts of evil things are about to befall them. If they start on a journey they are certain there is going to be a wreck. If a telegram comes, it is sure to contain some dreadful tidings. If a child seems a little quiet, the worrying mother is positive it is going to fall ill and die. If the husband seems thoughtful, as he revolves some business plan in his mind, then the good wife is convinced that he is beginning to cease to love her, and indulges in a crying spell. And so it goes - worry, worry, worry - each indulgence making the habit more at home.

After a while the continued thought shows itself in action. Not only is the mind poisoned by the blue thoughts, but the forehead shows deep lines between the eyebrows, and the voice takes on that whining, rasping tone so common among worry-burdened people.

Develop Your Latent Paranormal Powers

The condition of mind known as "fault-finding" is another emotion that grows fat with exercise. First, fault is found with this thing, then with that, and finally with everything. The person becomes a chronic "nagger" - a burden to friends and relatives, and a thing to be avoided by outsiders. Women make the greatest naggers. Not because men are any better, but simply because a man nagger apt to have the habit knocked out of him by other men who will not stand his nonsense - he find that he is making things too hot for himself and he reforms; while a woman has more of a chance to indulge in the habit. But this nagging is all a matter of habit. It grows from small beginnings, and each time it is indulged in it throws out another root, branch, or tendril, and fastens itself the closer to the one who has given it soil in which to grow.

Envy, uncharitableness, gossip scandal-mongering, are all habits of this kind. The seeds are in every human breast, and only need good soil and a little watering to become lusty and strong.

Each time you give way to one of these negative emotions, the easier do you make it for a recurrence of the same thing, or similar ones. Sometimes by encouraging one unworthy emotion, you find that you have given room for the growth of a whole family of these mental weeds.

Now, this is not a good old orthodox preachment against the sin of bad thoughts. It is merely a calling of your attention to the law underlying the psychology of emotion. Nothing new about it - old as the hills - so old that many of us have forgotten all about it.

If you wish to manifest these constantly disagreeable and unpleasant traits, and to suffer the unhappiness that comes from them, by all means do so - that is your own business, and privilege. It's none of mine, and I am not preaching at you - it keeps me busy minding my own business and keeping an eye on my own undesirable habits and actions. I am merely telling you the law regarding the matter, and you may do the rest. If you wish to choke out these habits, there are two ways open to you. First, whenever you find yourself indulging in a negative thought or feeling, take right hold of it and say to it firmly, and vigorously, "Get out!" It won't like this at first, and will bridle up, curve its back and snarl like an offended cat. But never mind - just say, "Scat" to it. The next time it will not be so confident and aggressive - it will have manifested a little of the fear-habit. Each time you repress and choke out a tendency of this kind, the weaker it will become, and the stronger will your will be.

Professor James says: "Refuse to express a passion, and it dies. Count ten before venting your anger, and its occasion seems ridiculous. Whistling to keep up courage is no mere figure of speech. On the other hand, sit all day in a moping posture, sigh, and reply to everything with a dismal voice, and your melancholy lingers. There is no more valuable precept in moral education than this, as all who have experience know: if we wish to conquer emotional tendencies in ourselves, we must assiduously, and in the first instance, cold-bloodedly, go through the outward movements of those contrary dispositions we prefer to cultivate.

Smooth the brow, brighten the eye, contract the dorsal rather than the ventral aspect of the frame, and speak in a major key, pass the genial compliment, and your heart must be frigid indeed if it does not gradually thaw.

I have spoken of the plan of getting rid of undesirable states of feeling by driving them out. But a far better way is to cultivate the feeling or emotion directly opposed to the one you wish to eradicate.

We are very apt to regard ourselves as the creatures of our emotions and feelings, and to fancy that these feelings and emotions are "we." But such is far from being the truth. It is true that the majority of the race are slaves of their emotions and feelings, and are governed by them to a great degree. They think that feelings are things that rule one and from which one cannot free himself, and so they cease to rebel. They yield to the feeling without question, although they may know that the emotion or mental trait is calculated to injure them, and to bring unhappiness and failure instead of happiness and success. They say, "We are made that way," and let it go at that.

The new Psychology is teaching the people better things. It tells them that they are masters of their emotions and feelings, instead of being their slaves. It tells them that brain-cells may be developed that will manifest along desirable lines, and that the old brain-cells that have been manifesting so unpleasantly may be placed on the retired list, and allowed to atrophy from want of use. People may make themselves over, and change their entire natures. This is not mere idle theory, but is a working fact which has been demonstrated by thousands of people, and which is coming more and more before the attention of the race.

No matter what theory of mind we entertain, we must admit that the brain is the organ and instrument of the mind, in our present state of existence, at least, and that the brain must be considered in this matter. The brain is like a wonderful musical instrument, having millions of keys, upon which we may play innumerable combinations of sounds. We come into the world with certain tendencies, temperaments, and pre-dispositions, We may account for these tendencies by heredity, or we may account for them upon theories of pre-existence, but the facts remain the same. Certain keys seem to respond to our touch more easily than others. Certain notes seem to sound forth as the current of circumstances sweeps over the strings. And certain other notes are less easily vibrated. But we find that if we but make an effort of the will to restrain the utterance of some of these easily sounded strings, they will grow more difficult to sound, and less liable to be stirred by the passing breeze. And if we will pay attention to some of the other strings that have not been giving forth a clear tone, we will soon get them in good working order; their notes will chime forth clear and vibrant, and will drown the less pleasant sounds.

We have millions of unused brain-cells awaiting our cultivation. We are using but a few of them, and some of these we are working to death. We are able to give some of these cells a rest, by using other cells. The brain may be trained and cultivated in a manner incredible to one who has not looked into the subject. Mental attitudes may be acquired and cultivated, changed and discarded, at will. There is no longer any excuse for people manifesting unpleasant and harmful mental states. We have the remedy in our own hands.

We acquire habits of thought, feeling, and action, repeated use. We may be born with a tendency in a certain direction, or we may acquire tendencies by suggestions from other; such as the examples of those around us, suggestions from reading, listening to teachers. We are a bundle of mental habits. Each time we indulge in an undesirable thought or habit, the easier does it become for us to repeat that thought or action.

Mental scientists are in the habit of speaking of desirable thoughts or mental attitudes as "positive," and of the undesirable ones as "negative." There is a good reason for this. The mind instinctively recognizes certain things as good for the individual to which it belongs, and it clears the path for such thoughts, and interposes the least resistance to them. They have a much greater effect than an undesirable thought possesses, and one positive thought will counteract a number of negative thoughts. The best way to overcome undesirable or negative thoughts and feelings is to cultivate the positive ones. The positive thought is the strongest plant, and will in time starve out the negative one by withdrawing from it the nourishment necessary for its existence.

Of course the negative thought will set up a vigorous resistance at first, for it is a fight for life with it. In the slang words of the time, it "sees its finish" if the positive thought is allowed to grow and develop; and, consequently it makes things unpleasant for the individual until he has started well into the work of starving it out. Brain cells do not like to be laid on the shelf any more than does any other form of living energy, and they rebel and struggle until they become too weak to do so. The best way is to pay as little attention as possible to these weeds of the mind, but put in as much time as possible watering, caring for and attending to the new and beautiful plants in the garden of the mind.

Develop Your Latent Paranormal Powers

For instance, if you are apt to hate people, you can best overcome the negative thought by cultivating Love in its place. Think Love, and act it out, as often as possible. Cultivate thoughts of kindness, and act as kindly as you can to everyone with whom you come in contact. You will have trouble at the start, but gradually Love will master Hate, and the latter will begin to droop and wither. If you have a tendency toward the "blues" cultivate a smile, and a cheerful view of things. Insist upon your mouth wearing upturned corners, and make an effort of the will to look upon the bright side of things. The "blue-devils" will set up a fight, of course, but pay no attention to them - just go on cultivating optimism and cheerfulness. Let "Bright, Cheerful and Happy" be your watchword, and try to live it out.

These recipes may seem very old and timeworn, but they are psychological truths and may be used by you to advantage. If you once comprehend the nature of the thing, the affirmations and autosuggestions of the several schools may be understood and taken advantage of. You may make yourself energetic instead of slothful, active instead of lazy, by this method. It is all a matter of practice and steady work. New Thought people often have much to say about "holding the thought;" and, indeed, it is necessary to "hold the thought" in order to accomplish results. But something more is needed. You must "act out" the thought until it becomes a fixed habit with you. Thoughts take form in action; and in turn actions influence thought. So by "acting out" certain lines of thought, the actions react upon the mind, and increase the development of the part of the mind having close relation to the act. Each time the mind entertains a thought, the easier becomes the resulting action - and each time an act is performed, the easier becomes the corresponding thought. So you see the thing works both ways - action and reaction. If you feel cheerful and happy, it is very natural for you to laugh. And if you will laugh a little, you will begin to feel bright and cheerful. Do you see what I am trying to get at? Here it is, in a nutshell: if you wish to cultivate a certain habit of action, begin by cultivating the mental attitude corresponding to it. And as a means of cultivating that mental attitude, start in to "act-out " or go through, the motions of the act corresponding to the thought. Now, see if you cannot apply this rule. Take up something that you really feel should be done, but which you do not feel like doing. Cultivate the thought leading up to it - say to yourself: "I like to do so and so," and then go through the motions (cheerfully, remember!) and act out the thought that you like to do the thing. Take an interest in the doing - study out the best way to do it - put brains into it - take a pride in it - and you will find yourself doing the thing with a considerable amount of pleasure and interest - you will have cultivated a new habit.

If you prefer trying it on some mental trait of which you wish to be rid, it will work the same way. Start in to cultivate the opposite trait, and think it out and act it out for all you are worth. Then watch the change that will come over you. Don't be discouraged at the resistance you will encounter at first, but sing gaily: "I Can and I Will," and get to work in earnest. The important thing in this work is to keep cheerful and interested. If you manage to do this, the rest will be easy.

I have spoken of the plan of getting rid of undesirable states of feeling by driving them out. But a far better way is to cultivate the feeling or emotion directly opposed to the one you wish to eradicate.

We are very apt to regard ourselves as the creatures of our emotions and feelings, and to fancy that these feelings and emotions are "we." But such is far from being the truth. It is true that the majority of the race are slaves of their emotions and feelings, and are governed by them to a great degree. They think that feelings are things that rule one and from which one cannot free himself, and so they cease to rebel. They yield to the feeling without question, although they may know that the emotion or mental trait is calculated to injure them, and to bring unhappiness and failure instead of happiness and success. They say, "We are made that way," and let it go at that.

The new Psychology is teaching the people better things. It tells them that they are masters of their emotions and feelings, instead of being their slaves. It tells them that brain-cells may be developed that will manifest along desirable lines, and that the old brain-cells that have been manifesting so unpleasantly may be placed on the retired list, and allowed to atrophy from want of use. People may make themselves over, and change their entire natures. This is not mere idle theory, but is a working fact which has been demonstrated by thousands of people, and which is coming more and more before the attention of the race.

No matter what theory of mind we entertain, we must admit that the brain is the organ and instrument of the mind, in our present state of existence, at least, and that the brain must be considered in this matter. The brain is like a wonderful musical instrument, having millions of keys, upon which we may play innumerable combinations of sounds. We come into the world with certain tendencies, temperaments, and pre-dispositions, We may account for these tendencies by heredity, or we may account for them upon theories of pre-existence, but the facts remain the same. Certain keys seem to respond to our touch more easily than others. Certain notes seem to sound forth as the current of circumstances sweeps over the strings. And certain other notes are less easily vibrated. But we find that if we but make an effort of the will to restrain the utterance of some of these easily sounded strings, they will grow more difficult to sound, and less liable to be stirred by the passing breeze. And if we will pay attention to some of the other strings that have not been giving forth a clear tone, we will soon get them in good working order; their notes will chime forth clear and vibrant, and will drown the less pleasant sounds.

We have millions of unused brain-cells awaiting our cultivation. We are using but a few of them, and some of these we are working to death. We are able to give some of these cells a rest, by using other cells. The brain may be trained and cultivated in a manner incredible to one who has not looked into the subject. Mental attitudes may be acquired and cultivated, changed and discarded, at will. There is no longer any excuse for people manifesting unpleasant and harmful mental states. We have the remedy in our own hands.

Develop Your Latent Paranormal Powers

We acquire habits of thought, feeling, and action, repeated use. We may be born with a tendency in a certain direction, or we may acquire tendencies by suggestions from other; such as the examples of those around us, suggestions from reading, listening to teachers. We are a bundle of mental habits. Each time we indulge in an undesirable thought or habit, the easier does it become for us to repeat that thought or action.

Mental scientists are in the habit of speaking of desirable thoughts or mental attitudes as "positive," and of the undesirable ones as "negative." There is a good reason for this. The mind instinctively recognizes certain things as good for the individual to which it belongs, and it clears the path for such thoughts, and interposes the least resistance to them. They have a much greater effect than an undesirable thought possesses, and one positive thought will counteract a number of negative thoughts. The best way to overcome undesirable or negative thoughts and feelings is to cultivate the positive ones. The positive thought is the strongest plant, and will in time starve out the negative one by withdrawing from it the nourishment necessary for its existence.

Of course the negative thought will set up a vigorous resistance at first, for it is a fight for life with it. In the slang words of the time, it "sees its finish" if the positive thought is allowed to grow and develop; and, consequently it makes things unpleasant for the individual until he has started well into the work of starving it out. Brain cells do not like to be laid on the shelf any more than does any other form of living energy, and they rebel and struggle until they become too weak to do so. The best way is to pay as little attention as possible to these weeds of the mind, but put in as much time as possible watering, caring for and attending to the new and beautiful plants in the garden of the mind.

For instance, if you are apt to hate people, you can best overcome the negative thought by cultivating Love in its place. Think Love, and act it out, as often as possible. Cultivate thoughts of kindness, and act as kindly as you can to everyone with whom you come in contact. You will have trouble at the start, but gradually Love will master Hate, and the latter will begin to droop and wither. If you have a tendency toward the "blues" cultivate a smile, and a cheerful view of things. Insist upon your mouth wearing upturned corners, and make an effort of the will to look upon the bright side of things. The "blue-devils" will set up a fight, of course, but pay no attention to them - just go on cultivating optimism and cheerfulness. Let "Bright, Cheerful and Happy" be your watchword, and try to live it out.

These recipes may seem very old and timeworn, but they are psychological truths and may be used by you to advantage. If you once comprehend the nature of the thing, the affirmations and autosuggestions of the several schools may be understood and taken advantage of. You may make yourself energetic instead of slothful, active instead of lazy, by this method. It is all a matter of practice and steady work.

New Thought people often have much to say about "holding the thought;" and, indeed, it is necessary to "hold the thought" in order to accomplish results. But something more is needed. You must "act out" the thought until it becomes a fixed habit with you. Thoughts take form in action; and in turn actions influence thought. So by "acting out" certain lines of thought, the actions react upon the mind, and increase the development of the part of the mind having close relation to the act. Each time the mind entertains a thought, the easier becomes the resulting action - and each time an act is performed, the easier becomes the corresponding thought. So you see the thing works both ways - action and reaction.

If you feel cheerful and happy, it is very natural for you to laugh. And if you will laugh a little, you will begin to feel bright and cheerful. Do you see what I am trying to get at? Here it is, in a nutshell: if you wish to cultivate a certain habit of action, begin by cultivating the mental attitude corresponding to it. And as a means of cultivating that mental attitude, start in to "act-out " or go through, the motions of the act corresponding to the thought. Now, see if you cannot apply this rule. Take up something that you really feel should be done, but which you do not feel like doing. Cultivate the thought leading up to it - say to yourself: "I like to do so and so," and then go through the motions (cheerfully, remember!) and act out the thought that you like to do the thing. Take an interest in the doing - study out the best way to do it - put brains into it - take a pride in it - and you will find yourself doing the thing with a considerable amount of pleasure and interest - you will have cultivated a new habit.

If you prefer trying it on some mental trait of which you wish to be rid, it will work the same way. Start in to cultivate the opposite trait, and think it out and act it out for all you are worth. Then watch the change that will come over you. Don't be discouraged at the resistance you will encounter at first, but sing gaily: "I Can and I Will," and get to work in earnest. The important thing in this work is to keep cheerful and interested. If you manage to do this, the rest will be easy.

WE have discussed the necessity of getting rid of fear, that your desire may have full strength with which to work. Supposing that you have mastered this part of the task, or at least started on the road to mastery, I will now call your attention to another important branch of the subject. I allude to the subject of mental leaks. No, I don't mean the leakage arising from your failure to keep your own secrets - that is also important, but forms another story. The leakage I am now referring to is that occasioned by the habit of having the attention attracted to and distracted by every passing fancy.

In order to attain a thing it is necessary that the mind should fall in love with it, and be conscious of its existence, almost to the exclusion of everything else. You must get in love with the thing you wish to attain, just as much as you would if you were to meet the girl or man you wished to marry. I do not mean that you should become a monomaniac upon the subject, and should lose all interest in everything else in the world - that won't do, for the mind must have recreation and change. But, I do mean that you must be so "set" upon the desired thing that all else will seem of secondary importance.

A man in love may be pleasant to everyone else, and may go through the duties and pleasures of life with good spirit, but underneath it all he is humming to himself "Just One Girl;" and every one of his actions is bent toward getting that girl, and making a comfortable home for her. Do you see what I mean? You must get in love with the thing you want, and you must get in love with it in earnest - none of this latter-day flirting, "on-today and off-tomorrow" sort of love, but the good old-fashioned kind, that used to make it impossible for a young man to get to sleep unless he took a walk around his best girl's house, just to be sure it was still there. That's the real kind!

And the man or woman in search of success must make of that desired thing his ruling passion - he must keep his mind on the main chance. Success is jealous - that's why we speak of her as feminine. She demands a man's whole affection, and if he begins flirting with other fair charmers, she soon turns her back upon him. If a man allows his strong interest in the main chance to be sidetracked, he will be the loser. Mental Force operates best when it is concentrated. You must give to the desired thing your best and most earnest thought.

Just as the man who is thoroughly in love will think out plans and schemes whereby he may please the fair one, so will the man who is in love with his work or business give it his best thought, and the result will be that a hundred and one plans will come into his field of consciousness, many of which are very important. The mind works on the subconscious plane, remember, and almost always along the lines of the ruling passion or desire. It will fix up things, and patch together plans and schemes, and when you need them the most it will pop them into your consciousness, and you will feel like hurrahing, just as if you had received some valuable aid from outside.

But if you scatter your thought-force, the subconscious mind will not know just how to please you, and the result is that you are apt to be put off from this source of aid and assistance. Beside this, you will miss the powerful result of concentrated thought in the conscious working out of the details of your plans. And then again the man whose mind is full of a dozen interests fails to exert the attracting power that is manifested by the man of the one ruling passion, and he fails to draw to him persons, things, and results that will aid in the working out of his plans, and will also fail to place himself in the current of attraction whereby he is brought into contact with those who will be glad to help him because of harmonious interests.

I have noticed, in my own affairs, that when I would allow myself to be side-tracked by anything outside of my regular line of work, it would be only a short time before my receipts dropped off, and my business showed signs of a lack of vitality. Now, many may say that this was because I left undone some things that I would have done if my mind had been centered on the business. This is true; but I have noticed like results in cases where there was nothing to be done - cases in which the seed was sown, and the crop was awaited. And in just such cases, as soon as I directed my thought to the matter the seed began to sprout.

I do not mean that I had to send out great mental waves with the idea of affecting people - not a bit of it. I simply began to realize what a good thing I had, and how much people wanted it, and how glad they would be to know of it and all that sort of thing, and lo! My thought seemed to vitalize the work, and the seed began to sprout. This is no mere fancy, for I have experienced it on several occasions; I have spoken to many others on the subject, and I find that our experiences tally perfectly. So don't get into the habit of permitting these mental leaks.

Keep your Desire fresh and active, and let it get in its work without interference from conflicting desires. Keep in love with the thing you wish to attain - feed your fancy with it - see it as accomplished already, but don't lose your interest. Keep your eye on the main chance, and keep your one ruling passion strong and vigorous. Don't be a mental polygamist - one mental love is all that a man needs - that is, one at a time.

Some scientists have claimed that something that might as well be called "Love" is at the bottom of the whole of life. They claim that the love of the plant for water causes it to send forth its roots until the loved thing is found. They say that the love of the flower for the sun causes it to grow away from the dark places, so that it may receive the light. The so-called "chemical affinities" are really a form of love. And Desire is a manifestation of this Universal Life Love. So I am not using a mere figure of speech when I tell you that you must love the thing you wish to attain.

Nothing but intense love will enable you to surmount the many obstacles placed in your path. Nothing but that love will enable you to bear the burdens of the task. The more Desire you have for a thing, the more you Love it; and the more you Love it, the greater will be the attractive force exerted toward its attainment - both within yourself, and outside of you.

YOU have noticed the difference between the successful and strong men in any walk of life, and the unsuccessful weak men around them. You are conscious of the widely differing characteristics of the two classes, but somehow find it difficult to express just in what the difference lies. Let us take a look at the matter.

Burton said: "The longer I live, the more certain I am that the great difference between men, the feeble and the powerful, the great and the insignificant, is energy and invincible determination - a purpose once fixed and then Death or Victory. That quality will do anything that can be done in this world - and no talents, no circumstances, no opportunities will make a two-legged creature a man without it." I do not see how the idea could be more clearly expressed than Burton has spoken. He has put his finger right in the center of the subject - his eye has seen into the heart of it.

Energy and invincible determination - these two things will sweep away mighty barriers, and will surmount the greatest obstacles. And yet they must be used together. Energy without determination will go to waste. Lots of men have plenty of energy - they are full to overflowing with it; and yet they lack concentration - they lack the concentrated force that enables them to bring their power to bear upon the right spot. Energy is not nearly so rare a thing as many imagine it to be. I can look around me at any lime, and pick out a number of people I know who are full of energy - many of them are energy plus - and yet, somehow, they do not seem to make any headway.

Develop Your Latent Paranormal Powers

They are wasting their energy all the time. Now they are fooling with this thing - now meddling with that. They will take up some trifling thing of no real interest or importance, and waste enough energy and nervous force to carry them through a hard day's work, and yet when they are through, nothing has been accomplished.

Others who have plenty of energy, fail to direct it by the power of the Will toward the desired end. "Invincible determination" - those are the words. Do they not thrill you with their power? If you have something to do, get to work and do it. Marshal your energy, and then guide and direct it by your Will - bestow upon it that "invincible determination" and you will do the thing.

Everyone has within him a giant will, but the majority of us are too lazy to use it. We cannot get ourselves nerved up to the point at which we can say, truthfully: "I Will. If we can but pluck up our courage to that point, and will then pin it in place so that it will not slip back, we will be able to call into play that wonderful power - the Human Will. Man, as a rule, has but the faintest conception of the power of the Will, but those who have studied along the occult teachings, know that the Will is one of the great dynamic forces of the universe, and if harnessed and directed properly it is capable of accomplishing almost miraculous things.

"Energy and Invincible Determination: -- aren't they magnificent words? Commit them to memory - press them like a die into the wax of your mind, and they will be a constant inspiration to you in hours of need. If you can get these words to vibrating in your being, you will be a giant among pygmies. Say these words over and over again, and see how you are filled with new life - see how your blood will circulate - how your nerves will tingle. Make these words a part of yourself, and then go forth anew to the battle of life, encouraged and strengthened. Put them into practice. "Energy and Invincible Determination" - let that be your motto in your work-a-day life, and you will be one of those rare men who are able to "do things."

Develop Your Latent Paranormal Powers

Many persons are deterred from doing their best by the fact that they underrate themselves by comparison with the successful ones of life, or rather, overrate the successful ones by comparison with themselves.

One of the curious things noticed by those who are brought in contact with the people who have "arrived" is the fact that these successful people are not extraordinary after all. You meet with some great writer, and you are disappointed to find him very ordinary indeed. He does not converse brilliantly, and, in fact, you know a score of everyday people who seem far more brilliant than this man who dazzles you by his brightness in his books. You meet some great statesman, and he does not seem nearly so wise as lots of old fellows in your own village, who waste their wisdom upon the desert air. You meet some great captain of industry, and he does not give you the impression of the shrewdness so marked in some little bargain-driving trader in your own town. How is this, anyway? Are the reputations of these people fictitious, or what is the trouble

The trouble is this: you have imagined these people to be made of superior metal, and are disappointed to find them made of the same stuff as yourself and those about you. But, you ask, wherein does their greatness of achievement lie? Chiefly in this: Belief in themselves and in their inherent power, in their faculty to concentrate on the work in hand, when they are working, and in their ability to prevent leaks of power when they are not working.

They believe in themselves, and make every effort count. Your village wise man spills his wisdom on every corner, and talks to a lot of fools; when if he really were wise he would save up his wisdom and place it where it would do some work. The brilliant writer does not waste his wit upon every corner; in fact, he shuts the drawer in which he contains his wit, and opens it only when he is ready to concentrate and get down to business. The captain of industry has no desire to impress you with his shrewdness and "smartness. He never did, even when he was young. While his companions were talking and boasting, and "blowing," this future successful financier was "sawin' wood and sayin' nuthin'."

Develop Your Latent Paranormal Powers

The great people of the world - that is, those who have "arrived" - are not very different from you, or me, or the rest of us - all of us are about the same at the base. You have only to meet them to see how very "ordinary" they are, after all. But, don't forget the fact that they know how to use the material that is in them; while the rest of the crowd does not, and, in fact, even doubts whether the true stuff is there. The man or woman who "gets there", usually starts out by realizing that he or she is not so very different, after all, from the successful people that they hear so much about. This gives them confidence, and the result is they find out that they are able to "do things." Then they learn to keep their mouths closed, and to avoid wasting and dissipating their energy. They store up energy, and concentrate it upon the task at hand; while their companions are scattering their energies in every direction, trying to show off and let people know how smart they are. The man or woman who "gets there," prefers to wait for the applause that follows deed accomplished, and cares very little for the praise that attends promises of what we expect to do "someday," or an exhibition of "smartness" without works.

One of the reasons that people who are thrown in with successful men often manifest success themselves, is that they are able to watch the successful man and sort of "catch the trick" of his greatness. They see that he is an everyday sort of man, but that he thoroughly believes in himself, and also that he does not waste energy, but reserves all his force for the actual tasks before him. And, profiting by example, they start to work and put the lesson into practice in their own lives.

Now what is the moral of this talk? Simply this: Don't undervalue yourself, or overvalue others. Realize that you are made of good stuff, and that locked within your mind are many good things. Then get to work and unfold those good things, and make something out of that good stuff. Do this by attention to the things before you, and by giving to each the best that is in you, knowing that plenty of more good things are in you ready for the fresh tasks that will come. Put the best of yourself into the undertaking on hand, and do not cheat the present task in favor of some future one. Your supply is inexhaustible. And don't waste your good stuff on the crowd of gapers, watchers and critics who are standing around watching you work. Save your good stuff for your job, and don't be in too much of a hurry for applause. Save up your good thoughts for "copy" if you are a writer; save up your bright schemes for actual practice, if you are a business man; save up your wisdom for occasion, if you are a statesman; and, in each case, avoid the desire to scatter your pears before - well, before the gaping crowd that wants to be entertained by a "free show."

Nothing very "high" about this teaching, perhaps, but it is what many of you need very much. Stop fooling, and get down to business. Stop wasting good raw material, and start to work making something worthwhile.

IN a recent conversation, I was telling a woman to pluck up courage and to reach out for a certain good thing for which she had been longing for many years, and which, at last, appeared to be in sight. I told her that it looked as if her desire was about to be gratified - that the Law of Attraction was bringing it to her. She lacked faith, and kept on repeating, "Oh! It's too good to be true - it's too good for me! She had not emerged from the worm-of-the-dust stage, and although she was in sight of the Promised Land she refused to enter it because it "was too good for her." l think I succeeded in putting sufficient "ginger" into her to enable her to claim her own, for the last reports indicate that she is taking possession.

But that is not what I wish to tell you. I want to call your attention to the fact that nothing is too good for YOU - no matter how great the thing may be - no matter how undeserving you may seem to be. You are entitled to the best there is, for it is your direct inheritance. So don't be afraid to ask - demand - and take. The good things of the world are not the portion of any favored sons. They belong to all, but they come only to those who are wise enough to recognize that the good things are theirs by right, and who are sufficiently courageous to reach out for them. Many good things are lost for want of the asking. Many splendid things are lost to you because of your feeling that you are unworthy of them. Many great things are lost to you because you lack the confidence and courage to demand and take possession of them.

"None but the brave deserves the fair," says the old adage, and the rule is true in all lines of human effort. If you keep on repeating that you are unworthy of the good thing - that it is too good for you - the Law will be apt to take you at your word and believe what you say. That's a peculiar thing about the Law - it believes - what you say - it takes you in earnest. So beware what you say to it, for it will be apt to give credence. Say to it that you are worthy of the best there is, and that there is nothing too good for you, and you will be likely to have the Law take you in earnest, and say, "I guess he is right; I'm going to give him the whole bakeshop if he wants it - he knows his rights, and what's the use of trying to deny it to him?" But if you say, "Oh, it's too good for me! The Law will probably say, "Well, I wouldn't wonder but that that is so. Surely he ought to know, and it isn't for me to contradict him." And so it goes.

Why should anything be too good for you? Did you ever stop to think just what you are? You are a manifestation of the Whole Thing, and have a perfect right to all there is. Or, if you prefer it this way, you are a child of the Infinite, and are heir to it all. You are telling the truth in either statement, or both. At any rate, no matter for what you ask, you are merely demanding your own. And the more in earnest you are about demanding it - the more confident you are of receiving it - the more will you use in reaching out for it - the surer you will be to obtain it.

Strong desire - confident expectation - courage in action - these things bring to you your own. But before you put these forces into effect, you must awaken to a realization that you are merely asking for your own, and not for something to which you have no right or claim. So long as there exists in your mind the last sneaking bit of doubt as to your right to the things you want, you will be setting up a resistance to the operation of the Law. You may demand as vigorously as you please, but you will lack the courage to act, if you have a lingering doubt of your right to the thing you want. If you persist in regarding the desired thing as if it belonged to another, instead of to yourself, you will be placing yourself in the position of the covetous or envious man, or even in the position of a tempted thief. In such a case your mind will revolt at proceeding with the work, for it instinctively will recoil from the idea of taking what is not your own - the mind is honest. But when your realize that the best the Universe holds belongs to you as a Divine Heir, and that there is enough for all without your robbing anyone else; then the friction is removed, and the barrier broken down, and the Law proceeds to do its work.

I do not believe in this "humble" business. This meek and lowly attitude does not appeal to me - there is no sense in it, at all. The idea of making a virtue of such things, when Man is the heir of the Universe, and is entitled to whatever he needs for his growth, happiness and satisfaction! I do not mean that one should assume a blustering and domineering attitude of mind - that is also absurd, for true strength does not so exhibit itself. The blusterer is a self-confessed weakling - he blusters to disguise his weakness. The truly strong man is calm, self-contained, and carries with him a consciousness of strength which renders unnecessary the bluster and fuss of assumed strength. But get away from this hypnotism of "humility" - this "meek and lowly" attitude of mind. Remember the horrible example of Uriah Heep, and beware of imitating him. Throw back you head, and look the world square in the face. There's nothing to be afraid of - the world is apt to be as much afraid of you, as yell are of it, anyway. Be a man, or woman, and not a crawling thing. And this applies to your mental attitude, as well as to your outward demeanor. Stop this crawling in your mind. See yourself as standing erect and facing life without fear, and you will gradually grow into your ideal.

There is nothing that is too good for you - not a thing. The best there is, is not beginning to be good enough for you; for there are still better things ahead. The best gift that the world has to offer is a mere bauble compared to the great things in the Cosmos that await your coming of age. So don't be afraid to reach out for these playthings of life - these baubles of this plane of consciousness. Reach out for them - grab a whole fistful - play with them until you are tired; that's what they are made for, anyway. They are made for our express use - not to look at, but to be played with, if you desire. Help yourself - there's a whole shopful of these toys awaiting your desire, demand and taking. Don't be bashful! Don't let me hear any more of this silly talk about things being too good for you. Pshaw! You have been like the Emperor's little son thinking that the tin soldiers and toy drum were far too good for him, and refusing to reach out for them. But you don't find this trouble with children as a rule. They instinctively recognize that nothing is too good for them. They want all that is in sight to play with, and they seem to feel that the things are theirs by right. And that is the condition of mind that we seekers after the Divine Adventure must cultivate. Unless we become as little children we cannot enter the Kingdom of Heaven.

The things we see around us are the playthings of the Kindergarten of God, playthings which we use in our game-tasks. Help yourself to them - ask for them without bashfulness demand as many as you can make use of - they are yours. And if you don't see just what you want, ask for it - there's a big reserve stock on the shelves, and in the closets. Play, play, play, to your heart's content. Learn to weave mats - to build houses with the blocks - to stitch outlines on the squares - play the game through, and play it well. And demand all the proper materials for the play - don't be bashful - there's enough to go round.

But - remember this! While all this be true, the best things are still only game-things - toys, blocks, mats, cubes, and all the rest. Useful, most useful for the learning of the lessons - pleasant, most pleasant with which to play - and desirable, most desirable, for these purposes. Get all the fun and profit out of the use of things that is possible. Throw yourself heartily into the game, and play it out - it is Good. But, here's the thing to remember - never lose sight of the fact that these good things are but playthings - part of the game - and you must be perfectly willing to lay them aside when the time comes to pass into the next class, and not cry and mourn because you must leave your playthings behind you. Do not allow yourself to become unduly attached to them - they are for your use and pleasure, but are not a part of you - not essential to your happiness in the next stage. Despise them not because of their lack of Reality - they are great things relatively, and you may as well have all the fun out of them that you can - don't be a spiritual prig, standing aside and refusing to join in the game. But do not tie yourself to them - they are good to use and play with, but not good enough to use you and to make you a plaything. Don't let the toys turn the tables on you.

This is the difference between the master of Circumstances and the Slave of Circumstances. The Slave thinks that these playthings are real, and that he is not good enough to have them. He gets only a few toys, because he is afraid to ask for more, and he misses most of the fun. And then, considering the toys to be real, and not realizing that there are plenty more where these came from, he attaches himself to the little trinkets that have come his way, and allows himself to be made a slave of them. He is afraid that they may be taken away from him and he is afraid to toddle across the floor and help himself to the others. The Master knows that all are his for the asking. He demands that which he needs from day to day, and does not worry about over-loading himself; for he knows that there are "lots more," and that he cannot be cheated out of them. He plays, and plays well, and has a good time in the play - and he learns his Kindergarten lessons in the playing. But he does not become too much attached to his toys. He is willing to fling away the worn-out toys, and reach out for a new one. And when he is called into the next room for promotion, he drops on the floor the worn-out toys of the day, and with glistening eyes and confident attitude of mind, marches into the next room - into the Great Unknown - with a smile on his face. He is not afraid, for he hears the voice of the Teacher, and knows that she is there waiting for him - in that Great Next Room.

SOME time ago I was talking to a man about the Attractive Power of Thought. He said that he did not believe that Thought could attract anything to him, and that it was all a matter of luck. He had found, he said, that ill luck relentlessly pursued him, and that everything he touched went wrong. It always had, and always would, and he had grown to expect it. When he undertook a new thing he knew beforehand that it would go wrong and that no good would come of it. Oh, no! There wasn't anything in the theory of Attractive Thought, so far as he could see; it was all a matter of luck!

This man failed to see that by his own confession he was giving a most convincing argument in favor of the Law of Attraction. He was testifying that he was always expecting things to go wrong, and that they always came about as he expected. He was a magnificent illustration of the Law of Attraction - but he didn't know it, and no argument seemed to make the matter clear to him. He was "up against it," and there was no way out of it - he always expected the ill luck. and every occurrence proved that he was right, and that the Mental Science position was all nonsense.

There are many people who seem to think that the only way in which the Law of Attraction operates is when one wishes hard, strong and steady. They do not seem to realize that a strong belief is as efficacious as a strong wish. The successful man believes in himself and his ultimate success, and, paying no attention to little setbacks, stumbles, tumbles and slips, presses on eagerly to the goal, believing all the time that he will get there. His views and aims may alter as he progresses, and he may change his plans or have them changed for him, but all the time he knows in his heart that he will eventually "get there." He is not steadily wishing he may get there - he simply feels and believes it, and thereby sets to operation the strongest forces known in the world of thought.

The man who just as steadily believes he is going to fail will invariably fail. How could he help it? There is no special miracle about it. Everything he does, thinks and says is tinctured with the thought of failure. Other people catch his spirit, and fail to trust him or his ability, which occurrences he in turn sets down as but other exhibitions of his ill luck, instead of ascribing them to his belief and expectation of failure. He is suggesting failure to himself all the time, and he invariably takes on the effect of the autosuggestion. Then, again, he by his negative thoughts shuts up that portion of his mind from which should come the ideas and plans conducive to success and which do come to the man who is expecting success because he believes in it. A state of discouragement is not the one in which bright ideas come to us. It is only when we are enthused and hopeful that our minds work out the bright ideas which we may turn to account.

Men instinctively feel the atmosphere of failure hovering around certain of their fellows, and on the other hand recognize something about others which leads them to say, when they hear of a temporary mishap befalling such a one: "Oh, he'll come out all right somehow - you can't down him." It is the atmosphere caused by the prevailing Mental Attitude. Clear up your Mental Atmosphere!

There is no such thing as chance. Law maintains everywhere, and all that happens because of the operation of Law. You cannot name the simplest thing that ever occurred by chance - try it, and then run the thing down to a final analysis, and you will see it as the result of law. It is as plain as mathematics. Plan and purpose; cause and effect. From the movements of worlds to the growth of the grain of mustard seed - all the result of Law. The fall of the stone down the mountainside is not chance - forces which had been in operation for centuries caused it. And back of that cause were other causes, and so on until the Causeless Cause is reached.

And Life is not the result of chance - the Law is here, too. The Law is in full operation whether you know it or not - whether you believe in it or not. You may be the ignorant object upon which the Law operates, and bring yourself all sorts of trouble because of your ignorance of or opposition to the Law. Or you may fall in with the operations to the Law - get into its current, as it were - and Life will seem a far different thing to you. You cannot get outside of the Law, by refusing to have anything to do with it. You are at liberty to oppose it and produce all the friction you wish to - it doesn't' hurt the Law, and you may keep it up until you learn your lesson.

The Law of Thought Attraction is one name for the law, or rather for one manifestation of it. Again I say, your thoughts are real things. They go forth from you in all directions, combining with thoughts of like kind - opposing thoughts of a different character - forming combinations - going where they are attracted - flying away from thought centers opposing them. And your mind attracts the thought of others, which have been sent out by them conscious or unconsciously. But it attracts only those thoughts which are in harmony with its own. Like attracts like, and opposites repel opposites, in the world of thought.

If you set your mind to the keynote of courage, confidence, strength and success, you attract to yourself thoughts of like nature; people of like nature; things that fit in the mental tune. Your prevailing thought or mood determines that which is to be drawn toward you - picks out your mental bedfellow. You are today setting into motion thought currents which will in time attract toward your thoughts, people and conditions in harmony with the predominant note of your thought. Your thought will mingle with that of others of like nature and mind, and you will be attracted toward each other, and will surely come together with a common purpose sooner or later, unless one or the other of you should change the current of his thoughts.

Fall in with the operations of the law. Make it a part of yourself. Get into its currents. Maintain your poise. Set your mind to the keynote of Courage, Confidence and Success. Get in touch with all the thoughts of that kind that are emanating every hour from hundreds of minds. Get the best that is to be had in the thought world. The best is there, so be satisfied with nothing less. Get into partnership with good minds. Get into the right vibrations. You must be tired of being tossed about by the operations of the Law - get into harmony with it.

Develop Your Latent Paranormal Powers

If you enjoyed this book, ask for our free catalog.

Write to:

Global Communications

P.O. Box 753

New Brunswick, NJ 08903

Email: mrufo8@hotmail.com

www.conspiracyjournal.com

Develop Your Latent Paranormal Powers